Thesaurus Erotica

Teesa Mee

DEDICATION

To my husband for his everlasting devotion and inspiration (and his excellent Deep-V Diver).

Warning: This book is strictly for adult reading/use. Be forewarned if you are squeamish around crude or crass language. Otherwise, learn and enjoy!

CONTENTS

ACKNOWLEDGMENTS

I gleaned all of the entries in this book from the internet. Many of the terms exist on several sites, so I have not identified where the verbiage originated. I used the following particular sites for my research and the full website addresses are located in my reference section: Google, Sex-Lexis, Urban Dictionary, and Online Slang Dictionary.

Thank you to Shelton Cole at SC Photos for my beautiful cover.

Also thanks to Angela Peters for the sex sound Thunderclap.

INTRODUCTION

Being a voracious reader, I have learned to love language. The English language has over a million words (Global Language Monitor, 2012), and yet we choose to use only a fraction of them in our daily conversations, writings, and reading. I have found this to be true especially in the world of romance and erotic literature. Authors make use of the same few words or euphemisms for sexual organs and sexual acts. My hope is that this book will allow writers to swell their sexual vocabulary and keep their readers intrigued and coming back for more (puns intended)!

DEFINITIONS

Noun: the name of a person, place, or object. Nouns are the subject and/or object in a sentence. For example, in the sentence "Joe hastily doinked the willing Mary," both Joe and Mary are nouns.

Verb: an action word; also called the predicate. In the above example, doinked is the verb.

Adjective: a descriptive word used with nouns. In the above example, willing is the adjective.

Adverb: a descriptive word used with verbs, adjectives, and other adverbs. In the above example, hastily is the adjective.

Euphemism: "a mild or pleasant word or phrase that is used instead of one that is unpleasant or offensive" (Merriam-Webster, 2014) . For use in this book, I label adjectives combined with nouns or adverbs combined with verbs as euphemisms.

1. FEMALE BODY PARTS

Abdominal Muscles

Terminology	Part of Speech
basement	Noun
chest	Noun
front exposure	Euphemism
midriff	Noun
midsection	Noun

Anus

Terminology	Part of Speech
A-hole	Euphemism
alleyway	Noun
asshole	Noun
back cave	Euphemism
back door	Euphemism
back end	Euphemism
back eye	Euphemism
back garden	Euphemism
back hole	Euphemism
back parlor	Euphemism
back passage	Euphemism
back porch	Euphemism
back slice	Euphemism
back slit	Euphemism
back way	Euphemism
back yard	Euphemism
back-door dirt box	Euphemism
backeye	Noun

Terminology	Part of Speech
backslice	Noun
backslit	Noun
backway	Noun
bakery goods	Euphemism
ballinocack	Noun
balloon knot	Euphemism
bang hole	Euphemism
barking spider	Euphemism
batty pipe	Euphemism
batty-hole	Noun
bazoo	Noun
bippy	Noun
blind eye	Euphemism
blot	Noun
blurter	Noun
bom	Noun
bomb bay	Noun
bosco boulevard	Euphemism
bottom	Noun
Bovril Bypass	Euphemism
brass eye	Euphemism
bronze eye	Euphemism
Brother round mouth	Euphemism
brown berry	Euphemism
brown bucket	Euphemism
brown bullet hole	Euphemism
brown cherry	Euphemism
brown daisy	Euphemism
brown eye	Euphemism
brown hole	Euphemism
brown house	Euphemism
brown star	Euphemism
brown Windsor	Euphemism

Terminology	Part of Speech
brown-eyed willy	Euphemism
brownie	Noun
Brunswick	Noun
bubble	Noun
bucket	Noun
buckeye	Noun
bum fiddle	Euphemism
bum hole	Euphemism
bun	Noun
bung	Noun
bunghole	Noun
bung-hole	Euphemism
butthole	Noun
caboose	Noun
cackpipe	Noun
Cadbury Avenue	Euphemism
Cadbury-alley	Euphemism
Cadbury-cul-de-sac	Euphemism
camera obscura	Euphemism
cave	Noun
change machine	Euphemism
change register	Euphemism
choccy	Noun
chocolate buttonhole	Euphemism
chocolate eye	Euphemism
chocolate highway	Euphemism
chocolate hole	Euphemism
chocolate road	Euphemism
chocolate speedway	Euphemism
chocolate starfish	Euphemism
chudini	Noun
chuff	Noun
chundini	Noun

Terminology	Part of Speech
chutney locker	Euphemism
cigar burn	Euphemism
clacker	Noun
coal hole	Euphemism
cocoa canal	Euphemism
codeye	Noun
coin slot	Euphemism
coops	Noun
cooz	Noun
cooze	Noun
copper penny	Euphemism
corn-dot	Euphemism
cornhole	Noun
council gritter	Euphemism
cozy drop	Euphemism
crapper	Noun
culo	Noun
cushion	Noun
dark ring	Euphemism
dark star	Euphemism
date	Noun
date locker	Euphemism
ditch	Noun
dokus	Noun
dopey	Noun
dot	Noun
doughnut	Noun
drain pipe	Euphemism
Elephant-and-Castle	Euphemism
exhaust pipe	Euphemism
eye of the ass	Euphemism
fantail	Noun
feak	Noun

Terminology	Part of Speech
fifth point of contact	Euphemism
foofer	Noun
freckle	Noun
fugo	Noun
Gary	Noun
Gary Glitter	Euphemism
gazoo	Noun
geegee	Noun
geegee hole	Euphemism
gig	Noun
giggy	Noun
gigi	Noun
gigi hole	Euphemism
gonga	Noun
gripples	Noun
grippley	Noun
ham flower	Euphemism
Hawaiian Eye	Euphemism
heinie highway	Euphemism
hind boot	Euphemism
Hinterland	Noun
hole	Noun
hoop	Noun
hymie	Noun
inner sanctum	Euphemism
jacksie	Noun
jam pot	Euphemism
jaxy	Noun
kazoo	Noun
keester	Noun
khali buttonhole	Euphemism
kiester	Noun
kootch	Noun

Terminology	Part of Speech
kwazakoo	Noun
little brown eye-ball	Euphemism
lovebub	Noun
love-bub	Euphemism
lovebud	Noun
love-bud	Euphemism
mahogany knot	Euphemism
marmite motorway	Euphemism
matako	Noun
monocular eyeglass	Euphemism
moon	Noun
muddy starfish	Euphemism
mudeye	Noun
mussy	Noun
mustard pot	Euphemism
north pole	Euphemism
o-ring	Euphemism
parlor	Noun
parlour	Noun
pervy	Noun
podex	Noun
poop chute	Euphemism
pooper	Noun
puckered brown eye	Euphemism
puckered starfish	Euphemism
purvy	Noun
quoit	Noun
rear	Noun
rear entry	Euphemism
rear-end	Noun
recky	Noun
rectum	Noun
red-eye	Euphemism

Terminology	Part of Speech
rinctum	Noun
ringpiece	Noun
ring-piece	Euphemism
rip	Noun
road less travelled	Euphemism
rocky road	Euphemism
rosebud	Noun
round brown	Euphemism
round pussy	Euphemism
rusty bullet hole	Euphemism
rusty bullet wound	Euphemism
rusty washer	Euphemism
second eye	Euphemism
servant's entrance	Euphemism
shit winker	Euphemism
shitter	Noun
sphincter	Noun
spice island	Euphemism
split	Noun
stank	Noun
starfish	Noun
stench trench	Euphemism
stink	Noun
Stinkhole Bay	Euphemism
tail gate	Euphemism
tail pipe	Euphemism
tailgate	Noun
tailpipe	Noun
tail-side	Euphemism
tan-track	Euphemism
the brown	Euphemism
The Hershey Highway	Euphemism
third eye	Euphemism

Terminology	Part of Speech
thrasher	Noun
Toblerone tunnel	Euphemism
trap two	Euphemism
tube	Noun
turd cutter	Euphemism
twatarooney	Noun
two-hole	Noun
wazoo	Noun
web-center	Euphemism
where the sun never shines	Euphemism
where-the-sun-don't-shine	Euphemism
wind mill	Euphemism
wind tunnel	Euphemism
windward passage	Euphemism
wing-wang	Euphemism
winker-stinker	Euphemism
winking walnut	Euphemism
winkle	Noun
workman's entrance	Euphemism
wrong door	Euphemism
ying-yang	Euphemism
yin-yang	Euphemism
you-know-where	Euphemism
zero	Noun

Arms

Terminology	Part of Speech
triceps	Noun

Breasts

Terminology	Part of Speech
air bags	Euphemism
apple dumplings	Euphemism
apples	Noun
appurtenances	Euphemism
assets	Noun
atom bombs	Euphemism
babaloos	Noun
babooms	Noun
baby bumpers	Euphemism
baby pillows	Euphemism
babys' dinners	Euphemism
bags	Noun
bags of mystery	Euphemism
bajongas	Noun
balcony	Noun
ballasts	Noun
balloons	Noun
baloobas	Noun
bamboochas	Noun
bangers	Noun
baps	Noun
barges	Noun
basket of goodies	Euphemism
bawangos	Noun
bazongas	Noun
bazonkers	Noun
bazookas	Noun
bazoomas	Noun
bazoombas	Noun
bazooms	Noun
bazoongas	Noun
bazoongies	Noun

Terminology	Part of Speech
bazumbas	Noun
bean bags	Euphemism
beanbags	Noun
beausom	Noun
beauties	Noun
beauts	Noun
bee stings	Euphemism
beef bags	Euphemism
begonias	Noun
bejonkers	Noun
bell peppers	Euphemism
bellys	Noun
berks	Noun
berthas	Noun
bezongas	Noun
bibble chunks	Euphemism
big brown eyes	Euphemism
big browneys	Euphemism
bikini fillers	Euphemism
bikini stuffers	Euphemism
blaaters	Noun
blamps	Noun
blinders	Noun
blossoms	Noun
blubber bags	Euphemism
blubbers	Noun
bobbers	Noun
bodacious tatas	Euphemism
bonbons	Noun
boob	Noun
boobies	Noun
boobifers	Noun
boobs	Noun

Terminology	Part of Speech
boobulars	Noun
boody	Noun
boom-booms	Noun
boosiasms	Noun
boosies	Noun
boovies	Noun
borsties	Noun
bosiasms	Noun
bosom	Noun
bosoms	Noun
boulders	Noun
bouncers	Noun
bra-busters	Euphemism
Brad Pitts	Euphemism
brassiere food	Euphemism
breastage	Noun
breasties	Noun
breastworks	Noun
bristen	Noun
Bristol bits	Euphemism
Bristol cities	Euphemism
Bristol City	Euphemism
Bristols	noun
brown eyes	Noun
bubatoes	Noun
bubbies	Noun
bubs	Noun
buckets	Noun
buddies	Noun
buddings	Noun
buds	Noun
buffers	Noun
bulbs	Noun

Terminology	Part of Speech
bumpers	Noun
bumpy jumpers	Euphemism
bunnies	Noun
bust	Noun
busters	Noun
busty	Adjective
butter bags	Euphemism
buxom	Adjective
buzwams	Noun
cabman's rest	Euphemism
cadabies	Noun
Café de Mama	Euphemism
cajooblies	Noun
cakes	Noun
cans	Noun
cantaloupes	Noun
carry a bundle	Euphemism
casabas	Noun
chalubbies	Noun
charleys	Noun
charlies	Noun
charmers	Noun
charms	Noun
chee-chees	Noun
cherries	Noun
cherry topped sundaes	Euphemism
chest and bedding	Euphemism
chest bunnies	Euphemism
chest flesh	Euphemism
chest pillows	Euphemism
chest puppies	Euphemism
chestnuts	Noun
chi-chis	Noun

Terminology	Part of Speech
chichitas	Noun
chones	Noun
chubbies	Noun
chumbawumbas	Noun
chungas	Noun
chupas	Noun
chussies	Noun
classy pair	Euphemism
coat hangers	Euphemism
female goodies	Euphemism
frontage	Noun
glands	Noun
globes	Noun
hangers	Noun
hooters	Noun
howitzers	Noun
hubbies	Noun
ivory hills	Euphemism
jaboos	Noun
jalobies	Noun
jellies	Noun
Jersey cities	Euphemism
jibs	Noun
jiggle bosoms	Euphemism
jigglers	Noun
jigglies	Noun
jobbies	Noun
jobblies	Noun
jubbies	Noun
jubblies	Noun
jubes	Noun
jublies	Noun
jugs	Noun

Terminology	Part of Speech
juicy peaches	Euphemism
jumbos	Noun
knick-knacks	Euphemism
knockers	Noun
marshmallows	Noun
milk jugs	Euphemism
nards	Noun
nick-nacks	Euphemism
pride and joy	Euphemism
sweets	Noun
swinger	Noun
tambourine	Noun
the baby bar	Euphemism
wobbly bits	Euphemism
yummies	Noun

Breasts and Buttocks

Terminology	Part of Speech
B & B	Euphemism
B and B	Euphemism
bees and bees	Euphemism

Breasts and Vagina

Terminology	Part of Speech
bubbies and cunt	Euphemism

Buttocks

Terminology	Part of Speech
A double S	Euphemism
after part	Euphemism
after parts	Euphemism
afters	Noun
apple bottom	Euphemism
ass	Noun
back	Noun
back end	Euphemism
back pack	Euphemism
back parlor	Euphemism
back part	Euphemism
back parts	Euphemism
back seat	Euphemism
back yard	Euphemism
backland	Noun
backs	Noun
backside	Noun
badinkadink	Noun
badonkadonk	Noun
ballinocack	Noun
basement	Noun
batty	Noun
beam	Noun
beauns	Noun
beautocks	Noun
beauts	Noun
behind	Noun
bell	Noun
bim	Noun
biscuit	Noun
biscuits	Noun
blind cheeks	Euphemism

Terminology	Part of Speech
Blind Cupid	Euphemism
bohunkus	Noun
bom	Noun
bomb bay	Euphemism
bombosities	Noun
bomsey	Noun
bonbon	Noun
bonbons	Noun
boody	Noun
bootie	Noun
booty	Noun
bosom of the pants	Euphemism
bot	Noun
bottom	Noun
breech	Noun
broad smile	Euphemism
bubble butt	Euphemism
bubble yum butt	Euphemism
bucket	Noun
bum	Noun
bummy	Noun
bumper	Noun
bun	Noun
bun-bun	Noun
bunchy	Noun
buns	Noun
bunt	Noun
business class	Euphemism
butt	Noun
caboose	Noun
cake	Noun
cakes	Noun
can	Noun

Terminology	Part of Speech
canister set	Euphemism
Capital B	Euphemism
cheeks	Noun
chips	Noun
chudini	Noun
chundini	Noun
clunes	Noun
cushion	Noun
dadonkadonk	Noun
dairy air	Euphemism
derriere	Noun
donk	Noun
donque	Noun
dookie maker	Euphemism
duff	Noun
dumps	Noun
fanny	Noun
fatty	Noun
fundament	Noun
glute	Noun
gluteus maximus	Noun
hams	Noun
haunches	Noun
hunkers	Noun
juicy double	Euphemism
junk in your trunk	Euphemism
low countries	Euphemism
money maker	Euphemism
nates	Noun
onion	Noun
pancake	Noun
patootie	Noun
pooter	Noun

Terminology	Part of Speech
posterior	Noun
pressed ham	Euphemism
rear	Noun
rear end	Euphemism
rump	Noun
rump shaker	Euphemism
saddle	Noun
salt shaker	Euphemism
seat	Noun
spread	Noun
tail	Noun
tail end	Euphemism
tambourine	Noun
The Big A	Euphemism
thick	Noun
tooshy	Noun
tuchus	Noun
tuckus	Noun
tush	Noun
whatsis	Noun
whatsus	Noun
whatzis	Noun
whoopie cake	Euphemism

Clitoris

Terminology	Part of Speech
baby in the boat	Euphemism
bald man in a boat	Euphemism
bald man in the boat	Euphemism
bean	Noun
beauty spot	Euphemism

Terminology	Part of Speech
bell	Noun
boy in the boat	Euphemism
bud	Noun
budgie's tongue	Euphemism
button	Noun
cherry pit	Euphemism
Clint Toris	Euphemism
clit	Noun
clitoris	Noun
clitty	Noun
clown's hat	Euphemism
dingleberry	Noun
doorbell	Noun
dot	Noun
expressive button	Euphemism
female cock	Euphemism
fleshy excrescence	Euphemism
goal keeper	Euphemism
hot spot	Euphemism
jointess	Noun
little boy in the boat	Euphemism
little bud	Euphemism
little man in the boat	Euphemism
little man in the female navicula	Euphemism
little ploughman	Euphemism
little shame tongue	Euphemism
love bud	Euphemism
love button	Euphemism
man in the boat	Euphemism
nub	Noun
nubbin	Noun
peeping sentinel	Euphemism
praline	Noun

Terminology	Part of Speech
prawn of pleasure	Euphemism
rosebud	Noun
sensible part	Euphemism
sensitive spot	Euphemism
shame tongue	Euphemism
slit bit	Euphemism
spare tongue	Euphemism
sugared diamond	Euphemism
tastebud	Noun
tender button	Euphemism
trigger	Noun
usher of the hall	Euphemism

Clitoris and Vagina

Terminology	Part of Speech
dynamic duo	Euphemism

Genitalia - External

Terminology	Part of Speech
pudendum	Noun

Genitals

Terminology	Part of Speech
altar of hymen	Euphemism
altar of love	Euphemism
altar of pleasure	Euphemism
apparatus	Noun
baby maker	Euphemism

Terminology	Part of Speech
basket	Noun
basket of goodies	Euphemism
bat wings	Euphemism
bearded clam	Euphemism
bearded lady	Euphemism
bearded oyster	Euphemism
bearded taco	Euphemism
beauty spot	Euphemism
beaver	Noun
beef	Noun
below the navel	Euphemism
best part	Euphemism
between the legs	Euphemism
big V	Euphemism
bit of jam	Euphemism
bit of pork	Euphemism
boody	Noun
bottom in front	Euphemism
box	Noun
bread	Noun
bun	Noun
business	Noun
business end	Euphemism
cabbage	Noun
cabbage field	Euphemism
cabbage garden	Euphemism
cabbage patch	Euphemism
cake	Noun
can	Noun
carnal parts	Euphemism
cat with its throat cut	Euphemism
cauliflower	Noun
chat	Noun

Terminology	Part of Speech
cockles	Noun
concern	Noun
cookie	Noun
coozey	Noun
coozie	Noun
coozy	Noun
covered way	Euphemism
crackling	Noun
crotch	Noun
cut	Noun
cuzzy	Noun
dark paradise	Euphemism
down below	Euphemism
down there	Euphemism
essentials	Noun
fanny	Noun
female goodies	Euphemism
female organs of generation	Euphemism
female organs of reproduction	Euphemism
female pudendum	Euphemism
fish city	Euphemism
fish mitten	Euphemism
fish pond	Euphemism
front bum	Euphemism
front garden	Euphemism
front porch	Euphemism
fud	Noun
fudy	Noun
fun zone	Euphemism
fur burger	Euphemism
furburger	Noun
furry hoop	Euphemism
futy	Noun

Terminology	Part of Speech
fuzz burger	Euphemism
fuzzburger	Noun
garden	Noun
garden of Eden	Euphemism
geography	Noun
gorilla burger	Euphemism
great divide	Euphemism
hair pie	Euphemism
hairy magnet	Euphemism
hairy pipi	Euphemism
intimate bits	Euphemism
intimate parts	Euphemism
itching jenny	Euphemism
itchy places	Euphemism
Jeanette Talia	Euphemism
jewel	Noun
jewelry	Noun
jig	Noun
ladies' treasure	Euphemism
little Mary	Euphemism
little sister	Euphemism
love muscle	Euphemism
low countries	Euphemism
lowlands	Euphemism
lunchbox	Noun
masterpiece	Noun
meat	Noun
middle kingdom	Euphemism
minge	Noun
moot	Noun
Mount Joy	Euphemism
Mount Pleasure	Euphemism
moving parts	Euphemism

Terminology	Part of Speech
muffin	Noun
mutton	Noun
natural parts	Euphemism
natural places	Euphemism
naturals	Noun
naughty bits	Euphemism
naval base	Euphemism
necessaries	Noun
nether regions	Euphemism
nookey	Noun
nooky	Noun
noose	Noun
nothing	Noun
organ of generation	Euphemism
organ of reproduction	Euphemism
oyster	Noun
package	Noun
palace of pleasure	Euphemism
pan	Noun
pancake	Noun
parts below	Euphemism
parts of generation	Euphemism
parts of reproduction	Euphemism
pee maker	Euphemism
periwinkle	Noun
playing field	Euphemism
plaything	Noun
pleasurable underside	Euphemism
pleasure boat	Euphemism
pleasure garden(s)	Euphemism
pleasure ground(s)	Euphemism
pleasure place	Euphemism
p-maker	Euphemism

Terminology	Part of Speech
poontang	Noun
prat	Noun
pratt	Noun
private property	Euphemism
privates	Noun
promised land	Euphemism
pump	Noun
purse	Noun
puss	Noun
rose	Noun
rubyfruit	Noun
rude bits	Euphemism
rude parts	Euphemism
saddle	Noun
secret parts	Euphemism
secret works	Euphemism
secrets	Noun
smoo	Noun
southern hemisphere	Euphemism
sportsman's gap	Euphemism
sportsman's hole	Euphemism
taco	Noun
tail	Noun
temple of low men	Euphemism
tender box	Euphemism
tender trap	Euphemism
that there	Euphemism
thing	Noun
third base	Euphemism
tickleables	Noun
tidbits	Noun
tid-bits	Euphemism
tinderbox	Noun

Terminology	Part of Speech
Tom Cat	Euphemism
tool box	Euphemism
toy shop	Euphemism
treasure	Noun
tuna	Noun
tuna town	Euphemism
twidget	Noun
twitchet	Noun
undercarriage	Noun
underparts	Noun
unmentionables	Noun
upper holloway	Euphemism
wares	Noun
waterworks	Noun
whatchamacallit	Noun
whatsis	Noun
whatsit	Noun
whatzis	Noun
whidgey	Noun
whim	Noun
whisper pot	Euphemism
woman's privates	Euphemism
woman's privities	Euphemism
woo-woo	Noun
wound	Noun
wrinkle	Noun
yum yum	Euphemism
yum-yum cake	Euphemism
zatch	Noun

Hymen

Terminology	Part of Speech
bean	Noun
bride's pride	Euphemism
bride's proof	Euphemism
buster	Noun
cherry	Noun
cherry blossom	Euphemism
delicate tissue	Euphemism
doorkeeper	Noun
maiden ring	Euphemism
tail gate	Euphemism
tailgate	Noun
virgin membrane	Noun
virginal membrane	Noun

Labia

Terminology	Part of Speech
bacon bomb doors	Euphemism
bacon rind	Euphemism
bacon strips	Euphemism
beef curtains	Euphemism
beef jibber	Euphemism
blood flaps	Euphemism
bovine drapes	Euphemism
breakfast of champions	Euphemism
bum bacon	Euphemism
cat flaps	Euphemism
columns of Venus	Euphemism
crevice	Noun
cunt lips	Euphemism
cuntocks	Noun

Terminology	Part of Speech
curtains	Noun
dangly bits	Euphemism
dew-flaps	Euphemism
double doors	Euphemism
double suckers	Euphemism
fish lips	Euphemism
flaps	Noun
flesh beer towels	Euphemism
front doors	Euphemism
fuck flaps	Euphemism
garden gates	Euphemism
great divide	Euphemism
hanging bacon	Euphemism
labs	Noun
lips	Noun
lower lips	Euphemism
meat tarp	Euphemism
ox drapes	Euphemism
palace gates	Euphemism
passion flaps	Euphemism
pink bits	Euphemism
pink flaps	Euphemism
portals of sex	Euphemism
scallops	Noun
sex skin	Euphemism
skins	Noun
slit	Noun
the butterflies	Euphemism
the rails	Euphemism
undercut	Noun
vaginal rim	Euphemism
vertical bacon sandwich	Euphemism
vulvar lips	Noun

Terminology	Part of Speech
wings of the vulva	Euphemism

Labia and Vagina

Terminology	Part of Speech
bacon	Noun
bacon sandwich	Euphemism
bawdy cleft	Euphemism
bilabial trump card	Euphemism
cleft	Noun
cleft of flesh	Euphemism
cleft underside	Euphemism
crease	Noun
female genital mouth	Euphemism
female genital slit	Euphemism
female gimcrack	Euphemism
female lower mouth	Euphemism
female pudendal slit	Euphemism
female slit	Euphemism
female's lower kisser	Euphemism
fillet o'fish	Euphemism
flabby lips	Euphemism
genital hiatus	Euphemism
genital slit	Euphemism
genital smile	Euphemism
Grand Canyon	Euphemism
grin	Noun
interlabial slit	Euphemism
joy furrow	Euphemism
lipped underside	Euphemism
lower mouth	Euphemism
mute mouth	Euphemism

Terminology	Part of Speech
pudendal smile	Euphemism
sexual slit	Euphemism
silent mouth	Euphemism
slitted underbelly	Euphemism
split	Noun
tram lines	Euphemism
tramlines	Noun
upright grin	Euphemism
upright wink	Euphemism
vertical bacon baguette	Euphemism
vertical smile	Euphemism
vulvar interlabial slit	Noun

Labia majora

Terminology	Part of Speech
outer labia	Noun
outer lips	Noun
outer vulvar lips	Noun

Labia minora

Terminology	Part of Speech
inner lips	Noun
inner vulvar lips	Noun
inside lips	Noun
minor lips	Noun
nymphae	Noun

Lips of the vulva

Terminology	Part of Speech
labia	Noun

Mons veneris and Labia

Terminology	Part of Speech
golden mound	Euphemism

Nipples

Terminology	Part of Speech
bee bites	Euphemism
bee stings	Euphemism
berries	Noun
bonbons	Noun
brown eyes	Euphemism
buds of beauty	Euphemism
button	Noun
buttons	Noun
cherries	Noun
cherrylets	Noun
headlights	Noun
jalobies	Noun
nub	Noun
nubbin	Noun
nubbins	Noun
nubs	Noun
tit-bits	Noun

Perineum – Female

Terminology	Part of Speech
barse	Noun
biffin bridge	Euphemism
biffits bridge	Euphemism
biffon	Noun
chin rest	Euphemism
chode	Noun
driving range	Euphemism
Duffy's bridge	Euphemism
gooch	Noun
nifkin	Noun
nifkin's bridge	Euphemism
stinkers bridge	Euphemism
taint	Noun
twitter	Noun
womfer	Noun

Pubic Hair

Terminology	Part of Speech
Apostle's grove	Euphemism
bear trapper's hat	Euphemism
beard	Noun
beard flit	Euphemism
bearded	Adjective
beaver	Noun
belly bristles	Euphemism
belly thicket	Euphemism
belly whiskers	Euphemism
Bermuda triangle	Euphemism
bird's nest	Euphemism
blurtbeard	Noun

Terminology	Part of Speech
briar patch	Euphemism
Brillo pad	Euphemism
brush	Noun
bush	Noun
carpet	Noun
clover field	Euphemism
cluster	Noun
cotton	Noun
cotton and wool	Euphemism
cunt carpet	Euphemism
cunt down	Euphemism
cunt hair	Euphemism
curlies	Noun
curls	Noun
curly hairs	Noun
delta	Noun
down	Noun
fascinating furpiece	Euphemism
fleece	Noun
forest	Noun
forest bush	Euphemism
Fort Bushy	Euphemism
frizzle	Noun
front garden	Euphemism
front-door mat	Euphemism
fuck fur	Euphemism
Fur	Noun
fur below	Euphemism
fur burger	Euphemism
furburger	Noun
furry bush	Euphemism
furry mound	Euphemism
furze	Noun

Terminology	Part of Speech
furze bush	Euphemism
fuzz	Noun
fuzz burger	Euphemism
fuzzburger	Noun
fuzzies	Noun
dickweed	Noun
garden	Noun
garden hedge	Euphemism
garden of Eden	Euphemism
goatee	Noun
gooseberry bush	Euphemism
gorilla burger	Euphemism
gorilla salad	Euphemism
grass	Noun
hairy pipi	Euphemism
kitten's ear	Euphemism
lawn	Noun
leg beard	Euphemism
lower wig	Euphemism
map of Tasmania	Euphemism
map of Tazzy	Euphemism
mat	Noun
moss	Noun
mossy doughnut	Euphemism
mound	Noun
mowed lawn	Euphemism
Old Frizzle	Euphemism
patch	Noun
plush	Noun
pubes	Noun
puff	Noun
pussy	Noun
pussy beard	Euphemism

Terminology	Part of Speech
pussy cover	Euphemism
pussy hair	Euphemism
rosebush	Noun
rug	Noun
short and curlies	Euphemism
short hairs	Euphemism
snatch patch	Euphemism
snatch thatch	Euphemism
steel woolies	Euphemism
strawberry patch	Euphemism
tail-feathers	Euphemism
thatch	Noun
thicket	Noun
turf	Noun
twat fuzz	Euphemism
twat hair	Euphemism
twat mat	Euphemism
twat rug	Euphemism
velcro strips	Euphemism
wig	Noun
wool	Noun
woolies	Noun
wools	Noun

Pubic Hair and Genitals

Terminology	Part of Speech
hairy escutcheon	Euphemism
muff pie	Euphemism

Pubic Hair and Vagina

Terminology	Part of Speech
brown madam	Euphemism
fresh axe wound in a bear's back	Euphemism
hairy axe wound	Euphemism
pink palace in the Black Forest	Euphemism
vertical axe wound with sideburns	Euphemism

Pubic Hair and Vulva

Terminology	Part of Speech
parsley bed	Euphemism
parsley patch	Euphemism

Pubis

Terminology	Part of Speech
fern	Noun

Pubis and Vagina

Terminology	Part of Speech
black cat with its throat cut	Euphemism

Tongue

Terminology	Part of Speech
clack	Noun
clacker	Noun
clapper	Noun

Vagina

Terminology	Part of Speech
all pink on the inside	Euphemism
alley	Noun
aperture of bliss	Euphemism
artichoke	Noun
article	Noun
Aunt Maria	Euphemism
Aunt Mary	Euphemism
axe wound	Euphemism
baby chute	Euphemism
baby factory	Euphemism
bacon hole	Euphemism
banger hanger	Euphemism
bank	Noun
barge	Noun
bayonet wound	Euphemism
bearded leisure center	Euphemism
beaver tail	Euphemism
beaver trap	Euphemism
beef box	Euphemism
beefbox	Noun
bit of flesh	Euphemism
biter	Noun
black box	Euphemism
black hole	Euphemism
black mouth	Euphemism
black ring	Euphemism
black velvet	Euphemism
Blue Beard's closet	Euphemism
blurt	Noun
bore	Noun
bottomless pit	Euphemism
bower of bliss	Euphemism

Terminology	Part of Speech
box with teeth	Euphemism
boy hole	Euphemism
Buckinger's boot	Euphemism
bull ring	Euphemism
bull's eye	Euphemism
bush pie	Euphemism
button hole	Euphemism
buttonhole	Noun
C**T	Euphemism
canyon	Noun
carnal trap	Euphemism
cave	Noun
cavern	Noun
cerassie	Noun
C-food	Euphemism
Charley	Noun
Charley Hunt	Euphemism
Charlie	Noun
Charlie Hunt	Euphemism
chat	Noun
cheese factory	Euphemism
cheesecake	Noun
chochito	Noun
chocho gordo	Euphemism
chopped liver	Euphemism
chow box	Euphemism
circle	Noun
clam	Noun
clap trap	Euphemism
claptrap	Noun
cock hotel	Euphemism
cock's alley	Euphemism
cockwash	Noun

Terminology	Part of Speech
coffee house	Euphemism
coffee shop	Euphemism
coffeehouse	Noun
coin slot	Euphemism
colpyle	Noun
conchita	Noun
constable	Noun
cooch	Noun
crack of heaven	Euphemism
cranny	Noun
crevice	Noun
cunny	Noun
cunt	Noun
Cupid's alley	Euphemism
Cupid's furrow	Euphemism
cut up	Euphemism
C-word	Euphemism
cylinder	Noun
dead end street	Euphemism
dingleberry	Noun
dirty hole	Euphemism
divine scar	Euphemism
doodle sack	Euphemism
dormouse	Noun
doughnut	Noun
downy bit	Euphemism
downy cave	Euphemism
empty tunnel	Euphemism
end of the sentimental journey	Euphemism
envy city	Euphemism
evening socket	Euphemism
everlasting wound	Euphemism
fat rabbit	Euphemism

Terminology	Part of Speech
female coital apparatus	Euphemism
female genital appeaser	Euphemism
female genital inlet	Euphemism
female genital passage	Euphemism
female genital receptacle	Euphemism
female gewgaw	Euphemism
female gew-gaw	Euphemism
female hiatus	Euphemism
female interlabial oven	Euphemism
female netherland	Euphemism
female organ of generation	Euphemism
female organ of reproduction	Euphemism
female perineal cul-de-sac	Euphemism
female pudendal canal	Euphemism
female pudendal chamber	Euphemism
female pudendal funnel	Euphemism
female pudendal gimcrack	Euphemism
female pudendal hawsehole	Euphemism
female pudendal inlet	Euphemism
female sex organ	Euphemism
female sexual organ	Euphemism
female sexual organon	Euphemism
female underbelly	Euphemism
figa	Noun
finger pie	Euphemism
fireplace	Noun
fish box	Euphemism
flange	Noun
flat cock	Euphemism
flat tail	Euphemism
flesh wallet	Euphemism
flounder	Noun
fly cage	Euphemism

Terminology	Part of Speech
fool trap	Euphemism
front attic	Euphemism
front bottom	Euphemism
front door	Euphemism
front entrance	Euphemism
front parlor	Euphemism
front passage	Euphemism
front room	Euphemism
front window	Euphemism
fuck hatch	Euphemism
fuck hole	Euphemism
fuckhole	Noun
fuck-hole	Euphemism
funk hole	Euphemism
funny bit	Euphemism
fur chalice	Euphemism
furrow	Noun
furry letterbox	Euphemism
furry mongoose	Euphemism
futz	Noun
fuzzy cup	Euphemism
fuzzy muzzy	Euphemism
G	Noun
gap	Noun
garage	Noun
gash	Noun
gasp and grunt	Euphemism
gee	Noun
generating place	Euphemism
genital chamber	Euphemism
gib tenuck	Euphemism
giggy	Noun
gim crack	Euphemism

Terminology	Part of Speech
gimcrack	Noun
ginch	Noun
glory hole	Euphemism
glue pot	Euphemism
gluepot	Noun
gold mine	Euphemism
golden doughnut	Euphemism
gorilla burger	Euphemism
grasp and grunt	Euphemism
grease box	Euphemism
greasebox	Noun
greedy pussy lips	Euphemism
groan and grunt	Euphemism
grotto	Noun
growl and grunt	Euphemism
growler	Noun
grumble	Noun
grumble and grunt	Euphemism
gut entrance	Euphemism
hair pie	Euphemism
hairy lasso	Euphemism
hairy Mary	Euphemism
hanging basket	Euphemism
happy hunting grounds	Euphemism
hatch	Noun
hatchway	Noun
heaven	Noun
heaven's porthole	Euphemism
hee	Noun
hidden treasure	Euphemism
hirsute oyster	Euphemism
ho cake	Euphemism
hole	Noun

Terminology	Part of Speech
Holiday Inn	Euphemism
home	Noun
home base	Euphemism
home sweet home	Euphemism
honey pie	Euphemism
honey pot	Euphemism
honeypot	Euphemism
hoohah	Noun
hoop	Noun
hot box	Euphemism
hotbox	Noun
inner sanctum	Euphemism
inner self	Euphemism
interlabial hiatus	Euphemism
interlabial sanctum	Euphemism
interlabial sanctum muliebre	Euphemism
itching jenny	Euphemism
jam donut	Euphemism
Jane	Noun
jelly bag	Euphemism
jelly box	Euphemism
jelly cave	Euphemism
jelly roll	Euphemism
jewel case	Euphemism
jimcrack	Noun
joxy	Noun
joy box	Euphemism
joy hole	Euphemism
joy spot	Euphemism
joy trail	Euphemism
juicy sewer	Euphemism
junioress	Noun
keyhole	Noun

Terminology	Part of Speech
kitty	Noun
kitty cat	Euphemism
knick-knack	Euphemism
lady flower	Euphemism
Lady Jane	Euphemism
lap land	Euphemism
lapland	Noun
Lili	Noun
lipped pudendal entrée	Euphemism
little kitten	Euphemism
little monkey	Euphemism
long eye	Euphemism
Lord knows what	Euphemism
Lord knows where	Euphemism
lotus	Noun
love box	Euphemism
love canal	Euphemism
love cleft	Euphemism
love glove	Euphemism
love grotto	Euphemism
love nest	Euphemism
love organ	Euphemism
love sheath	Euphemism
lovely flower	Euphemism
lowlands	Euphemism
main avenue	Euphemism
mama's box	Euphemism
man trap	Euphemism
man-eater	Euphemism
man-entrapment	Euphemism
manhole	Noun
man-hole	Euphemism
manometer	Euphemism

Terminology	Part of Speech
mantrap	Noun
mapatasi	Noun
Mary Jane	Euphemism
maw	Noun
melting pot	Euphemism
middle cut	Euphemism
middle eye	Euphemism
milk can	Euphemism
milk jug	Euphemism
milk pan	Euphemism
money box	Euphemism
money-pot	Euphemism
mouse trap	Euphemism
mouse's hole	Euphemism
mousetrap	Noun
mouth of nature	Euphemism
much-traveled highway	Euphemism
mustard pot	Euphemism
must-I-holler	Euphemism
mystic grotto	Euphemism
nappy dugout	Euphemism
night depository	Euphemism
nock	Noun
nook	Noun
nooker	Noun
notch	Noun
nursery	Noun
old hat	Euphemism
one that bites	Euphemism
open charms	Euphemism
open well	Euphemism
open wound	Euphemism
opening	Euphemism

Terminology	Part of Speech
organ grinder	Euphemism
orgasm chasm	Euphemism
oven	Noun
papaya	Noun
parlor	Noun
parlor room	Euphemism
parlour	Noun
passion hole	Euphemism
passion pit	Euphemism
peach-fish	Euphemism
pencil sharpener	Euphemism
phallic haven	Euphemism
pie	Noun
pink	Noun
pink eye	Euphemism
pink surprise	Euphemism
pink velvet sausage wallet	Euphemism
pit	Noun
pit of darkness	Euphemism
pit-hole	Euphemism
pit-mouth	Euphemism
playpen	Noun
pocketbook	Noun
pocket-book	Euphemism
poe	Noun
poke-hole	Euphemism
pole hole	Euphemism
pole vault	Euphemism
pond	Noun
poontenanny	Noun
pooz	Noun
poozie	Noun
poozle	Noun

Terminology	Part of Speech
portal of love	Euphemism
portal of Venus	Euphemism
pot	Noun
pouch	Noun
power U	Euphemism
premises	Noun
prime cut	Euphemism
pudendal hermitage	Euphemism
pudendal inlet	Euphemism
pudendal sanctum	Euphemism
punaani	Noun
punani	Noun
punanni	Noun
punni	Noun
puss	Noun
pussycat	Noun
quim	Noun
rag box	Euphemism
rat-hole	Euphemism
rattlesnake canyon	Euphemism
receiving chamber	Euphemism
receiving set	Euphemism
receptive pudendum	Euphemism
red ace	Euphemism
red lane	Euphemism
red snapper	Euphemism
rhubarb	Noun
road	Noun
road to heaven	Euphemism
road to paradise	Euphemism
road-to-a-christening	Euphemism
rocket socket	Euphemism
rotten crotch	Euphemism

Terminology	Part of Speech
Saint's delight	Euphemism
sanctum	Noun
sardine can	Euphemism
satchel	Noun
satin doll	Euphemism
scat	Noun
scratch	Noun
scum-twat	Euphemism
seafood	Noun
second hole from the back of the neck	Euphemism
sensible part	Euphemism
serpent socket	Euphemism
shake bag	Euphemism
sharp and blunt	Euphemism
she-thing	Euphemism
shmoy	Noun
shot-locker	Euphemism
sink of solitude	Euphemism
Sir Anthony Blunt	Euphemism
skin chimney	Euphemism
slash	Noun
sleeve	Noun
slice of life	Euphemism
slime hole	Euphemism
slippery slued	Euphemism
slit	Noun
sloppy bot	Euphemism
slot	Noun
smell-hole	Euphemism
smelly pussy	Euphemism
snackbar	Noun
snake pit	Euphemism

Terminology	Part of Speech
snapper	Noun
snapping pussy	Euphemism
snatch	Noun
snatch-blatch	Euphemism
snatch-box	Euphemism
snutchie	Noun
soft furry mound of love	Euphemism
south pole	Euphemism
spadger	Noun
sperm canal	Euphemism
sperm-sucker	Euphemism
spice of life	Euphemism
split tail	Euphemism
spread	Noun
spunk-pot	Euphemism
squeeky	Noun
squeeze box	Euphemism
squelchy monkey	Euphemism
stadge	Noun
staff-breaker	Euphemism
stank	Noun
stench trench	Euphemism
stink	Noun
stink hole	Euphemism
stink pot	Euphemism
stink well	Euphemism
stink-pit	Euphemism
stinkpot	Noun
sweet potato pie	Euphemism
tail box	Euphemism
tail for the cock	Euphemism
tail gap	Euphemism
tail gate	Euphemism

Terminology	Part of Speech
tail hole	Euphemism
tail pipe	Euphemism
tailgate	Noun
tailpipe	Noun
tee-tee	Noun
tenuc	Noun
that thing	Euphemism
The Beave	Euphemism
the damp	Euphemism
The Deep	Euphemism
the growl	Euphemism
the world's smallest hotel	Euphemism
thingstable	Noun
todger toaster	Euphemism
toolbox	Noun
toolshed	Noun
toot toot	Euphemism
toothless mouth	Euphemism
treasure box	Euphemism
treasury	Noun
tube	Noun
tuna fish	Euphemism
tunnel	Noun
tunnel of love	Euphemism
turnpike	Noun
twat	Noun
twelge	Noun
twixt wind and water	Euphemism
twot	Noun
upper holloway	Euphemism
V.D. depository	Euphemism
vacuum	Noun
vadge	Noun

Terminology	Part of Speech
vag	Noun
Vagina	Noun
vajajay	Noun
valley	Noun
valley of love	Euphemism
VD depository	Euphemism
velvet	Noun
velvet glove	Euphemism
velvet love canal	Euphemism
velvet tunnel	Euphemism
vent	Noun
Venus fly trap	Euphemism
Venus highway	Euphemism
vicious circle	Euphemism
vige	Noun
virgin treasure	Euphemism
Virginia Vagina	Euphemism
VJ	Noun
void	Noun
wad	Noun
warm fuzzy	Euphemism
warm place	Euphemism
warmest place	Euphemism
way-in	Euphemism
wet mop	Euphemism
whisker biscuit	Euphemism
whisker pot	Euphemism
whole	Noun
whole voyage	Euphemism
wonderland	Noun
yawn	Noun
yeast bag	Euphemism
yeast-mill	Euphemism

Terminology	Part of Speech
yellow road	Euphemism
YMCA	Euphemism
yoni	Noun

Vagina and Vulva

Terminology	Part of Speech
button groove	Euphemism
catty-cat	Euphemism
fount of feminity	Euphemism
fuzzy-bunny	Euphemism
golden gate	Euphemism
husband's supper	Euphemism
Irish fortune	Euphemism
kitty-cat	Euphemism
sunny south	Euphemism
thatch hatch	Euphemism
you know what	Euphemism

Vulva

Terminology	Part of Speech
cloven inlet	Euphemism
cloven spot	Euphemism
cooch	Noun
cunt pie	Euphemism
delta	Noun
female vulvar apparatus	Euphemism
front attic	Euphemism
front bottom	Euphemism
front door	Euphemism
front entrance	Euphemism

Terminology	Part of Speech
front parlor	Euphemism
front passage	Euphemism
front room	Euphemism
front window	Euphemism
hanging basket	Euphemism
peach	Noun
receptive pudendum	Euphemism
south pole	Euphemism
twat	Noun
twot	Noun
woo-woo	Euphemism
yoni	Noun

2. MALE BODY PARTS

Abdominal muscle

Terminology	Part of Speech
abs	Noun
basement	Noun
chest	Noun
front exposure	Euphemism
frontage	Noun
midriff	Noun
midsection	Noun
rectus abdominus	Noun
ripped	Adjective
six pack	Euphemism
washboard	Noun

Anus

Terminology	Part of Speech
A-hole	Euphemism
alleyway	Noun
arsehole	Noun
asshole	Noun
back cave	Euphemism
back door	Euphemism
back end	Euphemism
back eye	Euphemism
back garden	Euphemism
back hole	Euphemism
back parlor	Euphemism
back passage	Euphemism
back porch	Euphemism

Terminology	Part of Speech
back slice	Euphemism
back slit	Euphemism
back way	Euphemism
back yard	Euphemism
back-door dirt box	Euphemism
backeye	Noun
backslice	Noun
backslit	Noun
backway	Noun
bakery goods	Euphemism
ballinocack	Noun
balloon knot	Euphemism
barking spider	Euphemism
batty pipe	Euphemism
batty-hole	Euphemism
bazoo	Noun
bippy	Noun
blind eye	Euphemism
blot	Noun
blurter	Noun
bom	Noun
bomb bay	Euphemism
bosco boulevard	Euphemism
bottom	Noun
Bovril Bypass	Euphemism
brass eye	Euphemism
bronze eye	Euphemism
Brother round mouth	Euphemism
brown berry	Euphemism
brown bucket	Euphemism
brown bullet hole	Euphemism
brown cherry	Euphemism
brown daisy	Euphemism

Terminology	Part of Speech
brown eye	Euphemism
brown hole	Euphemism
brown house	Euphemism
brown Windsor	Euphemism
brown-eyed willy	Euphemism
brownie	Noun
Brunswick	Noun
bubble	Noun
bucket	Noun
buckeye	Noun
bum fiddle	Euphemism
bum hole	Euphemism
bun	Noun
bung	Noun
bunghole	Noun
bung-hole	Euphemism
butthole	Noun
caboose	Noun
cackpipe	Noun
Cadbury Avenue	Euphemism
Cadbury-alley	Euphemism
Cadbury-cul-de-sac	Euphemism
camera obscura	Euphemism
cave	Noun
change machine	Euphemism
change register	Euphemism
choccy	Noun
chocolate buttonhole	Euphemism
chocolate eye	Euphemism
chocolate highway	Euphemism
chocolate hole	Euphemism
chocolate road	Euphemism
chocolate speedway	Euphemism

Terminology	Part of Speech
chudini	Noun
chuff	Noun
chundini	Noun
chutney locker	Euphemism
cigar burn	Euphemism
clacker	Noun
coal hole	Euphemism
cocoa canal	Euphemism
codeye	Noun
coin slot	Euphemism
coops	Noun
cooz	Noun
cooze	Noun
copper penny	Euphemism
corn-dot	Euphemism
cornhole	Noun
council gritter	Euphemism
cozy drop	Euphemism
crapper	Noun
culo	Noun
cushion	Noun
dark ring	Euphemism
dark star	Euphemism
date locker	Euphemism
ditch	Noun
dokus	Noun
dopey	Noun
dot	Noun
doughnut	Noun
drain pipe	Euphemism
Elephant-and-Castle	Euphemism
exhaust pipe	Euphemism
eye of the ass	Euphemism

Terminology	Part of Speech
fantail	Noun
feak	Noun
foofer	Noun
fugo	Noun
Gary	Noun
Gary Glitter	Euphemism
gazoo	Noun
geegee	Noun
geegee hole	Euphemism
gig	Noun
giggy	Noun
gigi	Noun
gigi hole	Euphemism
gonga	Noun
gripples	Noun
grippley	Noun
growler	Euphemism
Hawaiian Eye	Euphemism
heinie highway	Euphemism
hind boot	Euphemism
Hinterland	Noun
hole	Noun
hoop	Noun
hymie	Noun
inner sanctum	Euphemism
jacksie	Noun
jam pot	Euphemism
jaxy	Noun
kazoo	Noun
keester	Noun
khali buttonhole	Euphemism
kiester	Noun
kootch	Noun

Terminology	Part of Speech
kwazakoo	Noun
little brown eye-ball	Euphemism
lovebub	Noun
love-bub	Euphemism
lovebud	Noun
love-bud	Euphemism
marmite motorway	Euphemism
matako	Noun
monocular eyeglass	Euphemism
moon	Noun
muddy starfish	Euphemism
mudeye	Noun
mustard pot	Euphemism
north pole	Euphemism
old dirt road	Euphemism
o-ring	Noun
parlor	Noun
parlour	Noun
pervy	Noun
podex	Noun
poop chute	Euphemism
pooper	Noun
prison purse	Euphemism
purvy	Noun
quoit	Noun
rear	Noun
rear entry	Euphemism
rear-end	Euphemism
recky	Noun
rectum	Noun
red-eye	Euphemism
rinctum	Noun
ringpiece	Noun

Terminology	Part of Speech
ring-piece	Euphemism
rip	Noun
road less travelled	Euphemism
rocky road	Euphemism
rosebud	Noun
round brown	Euphemism
round pussy	Euphemism
rusty bullet hole	Euphemism
rusty bullet wound	Euphemism
rusty washer	Euphemism
second eye	Euphemism
servant's entrance	Euphemism
shit winker	Euphemism
shitter	Noun
sphincter	Noun
spice island	Euphemism
split	Noun
stank	Noun
stench trench	Euphemism
stink	Noun
Stinkhole Bay	Euphemism
tail gate	Euphemism
tail pipe	Euphemism
tailgate	Noun
tailpipe	Noun
tail-side	Noun
tan-track	Euphemism
the brown	Euphemism
The Hershey Highway	Euphemism
third eye	Euphemism
thrasher	Noun
Toblerone tunnel	Euphemism
trap two	Euphemism

Terminology	Part of Speech
trouser trumpet	Euphemism
tube	Noun
turd cutter	Euphemism
twatarooney	Euphemism
wazoo	Noun
web-center	Euphemism
where the sun never shines	Euphemism
where-the-sun-don't-shine	Euphemism
wind mill	Euphemism
wind tunnel	Euphemism
windward passage	Euphemism
wing-wang	Euphemism
winker-stinker	Euphemism
winking walnut	Euphemism
winkle	Noun
workman's entrance	Euphemism
ying-yang	Euphemism
yin-yang	Euphemism
you-know-where	Euphemism
zero	Noun

Arms

Terminology	Part of Speech
biceps	Noun
guns	Noun
gunz	Noun
triceps	Noun

Buttocks

Terminology	Part of Speech
A double S	Euphemism
ace	Noun
after part	Euphemism
after parts	Euphemism
afters	Noun
arse	Noun
ass	Noun
back	Noun
back end	Euphemism
back pack	Euphemism
back parlor	Euphemism
back part	Euphemism
back parts	Euphemism
back seat	Euphemism
back yard	Euphemism
backland	Noun
backs	Noun
backside	Noun
ballinocack	Noun
basement	Noun
beam	Noun
beauns	Noun
beautocks	Noun
beauts	Noun
behind	Noun
bim	Noun
biscuits	Noun
blind cheeks	Euphemism
Blind Cupid	Euphemism
bohunkus	Noun
bom	Noun
bomb bay	Euphemism

Terminology	Part of Speech
bombosities	Noun
bomsey	Noun
bonbons	Noun
boody	Noun
bot	Noun
bottom	Noun
broad smile	Euphemism
bucket	Noun
bum	Noun
bummy	Noun
bun	Noun
bun-bun	Noun
bunchy	Noun
bunt	Noun
butt	Noun
cakes	Noun
canister set	Euphemism
chips	Noun
chudini	Noun
chundini	Noun
clunes	Noun
cushion	Noun
dookie maker	Euphemism
duff	Noun
glute	Noun
gluteus maximus	Noun
hams	Noun
haunches	Noun
heinie	Noun
keester	Noun
kiester	Noun
low countries	Euphemism
posterior	Noun

Terminology	Part of Speech
rear	Noun
rear end	Euphemism
rump	Noun
saddle	Noun
seat	Noun
spread	Noun
The Big A	Euphemism
tuchus	Noun
tuckus	Noun
tush	Noun
whatsis	Noun
whatsus	Noun
whatzis	Noun

Circumcised

Terminology	Part of Speech
chopped	Adjective
chopped-cock	Euphemism
clipped	Adjective
clipped dick	Euphemism
clipped-dick	Euphemism
cut	Adjective
cut-out-to-be-a-gentleman	Euphemism
kosher	Adjective
kosher-dill	Euphemism
kosher-style	Adjective
lop-cock	Euphemism
low-neck	Euphemism
low-neck-and-short-sleeves	Euphemism
nipped	Adjective
roundhead	Noun

Terminology	Part of Speech
short sleeved	Euphemism
skinned-back	Euphemism
snipped	Adjective
trimmed	Adjective
turtle-neck	Euphemism
twenty-twenty	Euphemism

Erection

Terminology	Part of Speech
a rise	Euphemism
awaken the bacon	Euphemism
bar on	Euphemism
battlefat	Noun
Bethelehem Steel	Euphemism
biological reaction	Euphemism
biological response	Euphemism
bit of hard	Euphemism
bit of stiff	Euphemism
boner	Noun
bone-up	Euphemism
bonk-on	Euphemism
get a stand	Euphemism
hard on	Euphemism
hard up	Euphemism
have it up	Euphemism
heat in the meat	Euphemism
hornification	Euphemism
morning hard on	Euphemism
morning pride	Euphemism
Mr. Priapus	Euphemism
packing heat	Euphemism

Terminology	Part of Speech
phallic decorum	Euphemism
piss hard	Euphemism
pitch a tent	Euphemism
pitching a tent in one's shorts	Euphemism
prick stand	Euphemism
purple throbber	Euphemism
raise a gallop	Euphemism
rise in the Levis	Euphemism
rock formation	Euphemism
rock python	Euphemism
rod-on	Euphemism
schwing	Noun
spiked phallus	Euphemism
sporting some wood	Euphemism
standing member	Euphemism
stemmer	Noun
stiff	Adjective
stiff deity	Euphemism
stiff on	Euphemism
stiff one	Euphemism
stiff peter	Euphemism
stiff prick	Euphemism
stiff stander	Euphemism
stuffy	Adjective
Sunday clothes	Euphemism
swelling	Noun
tail high	Euphemism
tent pole	Euphemism
throbbing member	Euphemism
throbbing muscle of pure love	Euphemism
throbbing python	Euphemism
thumper	Noun
touch-on	Euphemism

Terminology	Part of Speech
trouser tent	Euphemism
tumescence	Noun
tumescent	Adjective
turgid bayonet	Euphemism
Uncle Jim at attention and the twins	Euphemism
up	Adjective
up a bone	Euphemism
up-pointed male spike	Euphemism
upscope	Noun
virile reflex	Euphemism
wake up with Jake up	Euphemism
with his tail high	Euphemism
woody	Noun
Yasser	Noun
Yasser Crackafat	Euphemism

Foreskin

Terminology	Part of Speech
banana skin	Euphemism
blinds	Noun
bobby's anorak	Euphemism
café curtains	Euphemism
curtains	Noun
drapes	Noun
extra skin	Euphemism
goatskin	Noun
helmet pelmet	Euphemism
hood	Noun
lace	Noun
lace curtains	Euphemism

Terminology	Part of Speech
onion skin	Euphemism
prepuce	Noun
Principal Skinner	Euphemism
sheath	Noun
snapper	Noun
turtle neck sweater	Euphemism

Genitals

Terminology	Part of Speech
baggage	Euphemism
bagpipes	Noun
basketful of meat	Euphemism
bit of beef	Euphemism
cluster	Noun
credentials	Noun
forbidden zone	Euphemism
groceries	Noun
hardware	Euphemism
holiday money	Euphemism
kit	Noun
knick knacks	Euphemism
knick-knacks	Noun
loins	Noun
luggage	Noun
male netherlands	Euphemism
male organs of reproduction	Euphemism
male pudendum	Euphemism
male reproductive organs	Euphemism
manliness	Noun
marriage gear	Euphemism
meat and potatoes	Euphemism

Terminology	Part of Speech
mommy-daddy button	Euphemism
most precious parts	Euphemism
nasty bits	Euphemism
nick nacks	Euphemism
nick-nacks	Noun
nuts and bolts	Euphemism
pen and tassel	Euphemism
popular parts	Euphemism
tackle	Noun
three-piece set	Euphemism
three-piece suit	Euphemism
two dots and a dash	Euphemism
wobbly bits	Euphemism
wooter	Noun

Genitalia - External

Terminology	Part of Speech
pudendum	Noun

Glans-penis

Terminology	Part of Speech
acorn	Noun
bishop's mitre	Euphemism
bell	Noun

Muscles

Terminology	Part of Speech
cuts	Noun
iron-bound	Adjective
jacked	Adjective
pumped	Adjective

Nipples

Terminology	Part of Speech
brown eyes	Euphemism
nubbin	Noun

Penis

Terminology	Part of Speech
100% all -beef thermometer	Euphemism
a bit of hard for a bit of soft	Euphemism
a piece of meat	Euphemism
ABD (a big dick)	Euphemism
abominable pants worm	Euphemism
accoutrements	Noun
Accu-Jac	Euphemism
ace poker	Euphemism
adamantine organon	Euphemism
Adam's arsenal	Euphemism
Adam's whip	Euphemism
Adolph	Noun
Alabama black snake	Euphemism
albino cave dweller	Euphemism
all-beef sausage	Euphemism
anaconda	Noun
antenna	Noun

Terminology	Part of Speech
appendage	Noun
arm	Noun
Arm of justice	Euphemism
arm of love	Euphemism
arrow	Noun
auger	Noun
baby arm	Euphemism
baby beef	Euphemism
baby's arm	Euphemism
baby's forearm	Euphemism
bacon bazooka	Euphemism
bag of tricks	Euphemism
bald eagle	Euphemism
bald man	Euphemism
bald-headed candidate	Euphemism
bald-headed hermit	Euphemism
bald-headed mouse	Euphemism
bald-headed rat	Euphemism
bald-headed yogurt slinger	Euphemism
ballarat	Noun
baloney	Noun
baloney pony	Euphemism
bamboo stick	Euphemism
banana	Noun
band member	Euphemism
banger	Noun
bar	Noun
barge pole	Euphemism
basalisk	Noun
baton	Noun
batter	Noun
battering piece	Euphemism
battering ram	Euphemism

Terminology	Part of Speech
bauble	Noun
bazooka	Noun
bazooka shooter	Euphemism
BBC (big black cock)	Euphemism
BBD (big black dick)	Euphemism
BD drill	Euphemism
beak	Noun
bean	Noun
bean pole	Euphemism
bean shooter	Euphemism
bean tosser	Euphemism
beard splitter	Euphemism
beard-splitter	Euphemism
beating tool	Euphemism
beaver basher	Euphemism
beaver cleaver	Euphemism
beaver lever	Euphemism
bed flute	Euphemism
beef bayo with extra mayo	Euphemism
beef bayonet	Euphemism
beef in the can	Euphemism
beef jerky	Euphemism
beef stick	Euphemism
beef whistle	Euphemism
beer can	Euphemism
bell on a pole	Euphemism
bell rope	Euphemism
bell-knobbed	Adjective
bell-swagged	Adjective
belly ruffian	Euphemism
belongings	Noun
belt buster	Euphemism
bent stick	Euphemism

Terminology	Part of Speech
best friend	Euphemism
best leg of three	Euphemism
Bethlehem Steel	Euphemism
between you and me is the bed post	Euphemism
bicho	Noun
Big Cockatoo	Euphemism
big dipper	Euphemism
big hunk of meat	Euphemism
big one	Euphemism
big piece of meat	Euphemism
big red	Euphemism
big wand	Euphemism
bilbo	Noun
billy club	Euphemism
bird	Noun
bishop	Noun
blanket stiff	Euphemism
blind	Adjective
blind as a boiled turnip	Euphemism
blind Bob	Euphemism
blind buckler	Euphemism
blind meat	Euphemism
blind piece	Euphemism
blood breaker	Euphemism
blow pop	Euphemism
blow stick	Euphemism
blow torch	Euphemism
bludgeon	Noun
bludgin' koala basher	Euphemism
Blue Beard	Euphemism
blue steeler	Euphemism
blue thimble	Euphemism
blue vein	Euphemism

Terminology	Part of Speech
blue veiner	Euphemism
blue-veined custard chucker	Euphemism
blue-veined junket hooligan (or BVH)	Euphemism
blue-veined junket pump	Euphemism
blue-veined piccolo	Euphemism
blue-veined steak	Euphemism
blue-veined throbber	Euphemism
blue-veined trumpet	Euphemism
Bob Dole	Euphemism
bobby dangler	Euphemism
body captain	Euphemism
boinng	Noun
bomb head	Euphemism
bone	Noun
bone in the leg	Euphemism
boneless appendage	Euphemism
boneless fish	Euphemism
boneless stiff	Euphemism
boner	Noun
bookworm	Noun
boom stick	Noun
boomerang	Noun
boy toy	Euphemism
braciole	Noun
branch	Noun
brat-getter	Euphemism
bratwurst	Noun
broner	Noun
broom handle	Euphemism
broomstick	Noun
bruiser	Noun
bubbly jack	Euphemism

Terminology	Part of Speech
bubbly jock	Euphemism
bucking bronco	Euphemism
bud	Noun
buffing stick	Euphemism
bug-fucker	Euphemism
bulge	Noun
bull point	Euphemism
bullish	Adjective
bum tickler	Euphemism
bun puncher	Euphemism
bung	Noun
burrito	Noun
bush basher	Euphemism
buster	Noun
butcher	Noun
butt basher	Euphemism
butt smasher	Euphemism
butterfinger	Noun
buttom mushroom	Euphemism
button buster	Euphemism
cack	Noun
candy cane	Euphemism
candy-stick	Euphemism
cane	Noun
cannon	Noun
Captain Hard	Euphemism
Captain Hightop the Love Commander	Euphemism
Captain Hogseye	Euphemism
Captain Picard	Euphemism
Captain Standish	Euphemism
carnal member	Euphemism
carnal part	Euphemism

Terminology	Part of Speech
carrot	Noun
carry a big stick	Euphemism
Casey	Noun
cavity probe	Euphemism
Chairman Mao	Euphemism
charger	Noun
Charles the Bald	Euphemism
cherry assassin	Euphemism
cherry picker	Euphemism
cherry splitter	Euphemism
chibi	Noun
Chief of staff	Euphemism
chingus	Noun
choad	Noun
chooza	Noun
chopper	Noun
chub	Noun
chunky monkey	Euphemism
chut	Noun
club	Noun
cobra	Noun
Cock	Noun
cock on	Euphemism
cockaroony	Noun
cocked	Adjective
cocked gun	Euphemism
cockstand	Noun
cocktus erectus	Euphemism
cod	Noun
cold meat	Euphemism
command module	Euphemism
Compass of the Netherlands	Euphemism
concrete donkey	Euphemism

Terminology	Part of Speech
copper stick	Euphemism
corker	Noun
corn beef cudgel	Euphemism
cornholer	Noun
crab ladder	Euphemism
crack a fat	Euphemism
crack hunter	Euphemism
cracking tool	Euphemism
cracksman	Noun
cranny axe	Euphemism
cranny hunter	Euphemism
cream-stick	Euphemism
crimson chitterling	Euphemism
crimson crowbar	Euphemism
crotch cartilage	Euphemism
crotch cobra	Euphemism
crotch dachshund	Euphemism
crotch hunter	Euphemism
cucumber	Noun
cum gun	Euphemism
cunny catcher	Euphemism
cunt stabber	Euphemism
cunt stand	Euphemism
cunt stretcher	Euphemism
Cupid's torch	Euphemism
custard launcher	Euphemism
cut	Noun
cyclops	Noun
d	Noun
dagger	Noun
dawn horn	Euphemism
deep v diver	Euphemism
delight of women	Euphemism

Terminology	Part of Speech
derrick	Noun
diamond cutter	Euphemism
Dick	Noun
dick butkiss	Euphemism
dick smalls	Euphemism
dickie	Noun
dicktator	Noun
dicky bird	Euphemism
Diego the explorer	Euphemism
digitis erectus	Euphemism
ding dong	Euphemism
ding dong mcdork	Euphemism
dingaling	Noun
dingus	Noun
dink	Noun
dipstick	Noun
disco stick	Euphemism
dna rifle	Euphemism
doder	Noun
dog head	Euphemism
doinker	Noun
domepiece	Noun
Donald Pump	Euphemism
dong	Noun
donga	Noun
donger	Noun
donut holder	Euphemism
doodle	Noun
dork	Noun
dragon	Noun
drain pipe	Euphemism
drill	Noun
driving post	Euphemism

Terminology	Part of Speech
drum stick	Euphemism
D-train	Euphemism
dude piston	Euphemism
easy rider	Euphemism
eel	Noun
Egg leg	Euphemism
eggroll	Noun
egg-white cannon	Euphemism
ejac vac	Euphemism
elephant	Noun
elevator	Noun
eleventh finger	Euphemism
Elmer Pudd	Euphemism
enemy	Noun
engine of love	Euphemism
English sentry	Euphemism
enob or eenob	Noun
e-peen	Euphemism
erected spermapositor	Euphemism
erectivation	Euphemism
Eric Shun	Euphemism
everlasting gobstopper	Euphemism
excalibur	Noun
extra digit	Euphemism
eye dropper	Euphemism
fancy work	Euphemism
fang	Noun
ferret	Noun
fire hose	Euphemism
firm worm	Euphemism
fish stick	Euphemism
fixed bayonet	Euphemism
flagpole	Noun

Terminology	Part of Speech
flesh pencil	Euphemism
flesh tower	Euphemism
floppy drive	Euphemism
foaming beef probe	Euphemism
fool-sticker	Euphemism
foreman	Noun
formerly caged viper	Euphemism
fountain pen	Euphemism
Fred	Noun
frigamajig	Noun
froto	Noun
fuck rod	Euphemism
fuck stem	Euphemism
fuck stick	Euphemism
fuck truck	Euphemism
fud packer	Euphemism
fudge sickle	Euphemism
fun bone	Euphemism
fun stick	Euphemism
funk stick	Euphemism
funmaker	Noun
gadget	Noun
gadso	Noun
gapstopper	Noun
gardener	Noun
gator	Noun
gear	Noun
gearbox	Noun
gearshift	Noun
gearstick	Noun
gearstick d'amour	Euphemism
generating tool	Euphemism
generation tool	Euphemism

Terminology	Part of Speech
genital forefoot	Euphemism
genital pound of flesh	Euphemism
genital reamer	Euphemism
genital shaft	Euphemism
genital staff	Euphemism
gentle fist	Euphemism
gentle tittler	Euphemism
gentleman	Noun
gentleman's appendage	Euphemism
German helmet	Euphemism
get-it-up	Euphemism
gherkin	Noun
giggle stick	Euphemism
giggling pin	Euphemism
gigi	Noun
girl catcher	Euphemism
girlometer	Noun
glory pole	Euphemism
glossy rod of muscle and blood	Euphemism
glow rod	Euphemism
glow stick	Euphemism
gnarled root of love	Euphemism
gnat meat	Euphemism
gobstopper	Noun
Gods revenge on a woman	Euphemism
golden rivet	Euphemism
goober	Noun
good foot	Euphemism
goose's neck	Euphemism
goot	Noun
gravy maker	Euphemism
great Australian bite	Euphemism
grinding tool	Euphemism

Terminology	Part of Speech
gristle missile	Euphemism
groin	Noun
ground squirrel	Euphemism
guided missile	Euphemism
gun	Noun
gut wrench	Euphemism
hacker	Noun
hair divider	Euphemism
hair splitter	Euphemism
hairless wonder	Euphemism
hairy banana	Euphemism
hairy sausage	Euphemism
halfmast	Noun
ham howitzer	Euphemism
hambone	Noun
Hamilton Wick	Euphemism
hammer	Noun
Hampton Wick	Euphemism
handle	Noun
hand-made	Euphemism
hand-raised	Euphemism
hand-reared	Euphemism
hand-staff	Euphemism
hangdown	Noun
hanging meat	Euphemism
hard drive	Euphemism
hard head	Euphemism
hard salami	Euphemism
hard-bit	Euphemism
hardened spermapositor	Euphemism
Hardhat Harry	Euphemism
harpoon	Noun
hat rack	Euphemism

Terminology	Part of Speech
he tank	Euphemism
heat seeking missle	Euphemism
hermit	Noun
he-thing	Euphemism
hockey cocky	Euphemism
hodge dog	Euphemism
hoe-handle	Euphemism
hog	Noun
hogger	Noun
ho-handle	Euphemism
hole-puncher	Euphemism
hollow point	Euphemism
holy poker	Euphemism
holy wand	Euphemism
honker	Noun
honorable prick	Euphemism
hooded	Adjective
Hoover tower	Euphemism
hopping bug	Euphemism
horse's handbrake	Euphemism
hose	Noun
hot dog	Euphemism
hot member	Euphemism
hot pocket	Euphemism
hotchee	Noun
hugen	Noun
humpmobile	Noun
hung	Noun
hunk of meat	Euphemism
husbandman of nature	Euphemism
ice cream cone	Euphemism
ice cream machine	Euphemism
ID	Noun

Terminology	Part of Speech
idol	Noun
inch instrument	Euphemism
jack	Noun
jack in the box	Euphemism
jackalope	Noun
jackhammer	Noun
jacktool	Noun
jammy	Noun
jang	Noun
jawbreaker	Noun
jean tent	Euphemism
jelly roll	Euphemism
jenny	Noun
jigg	Noun
jigger	Noun
jiggle bone	Euphemism
jig-jag	Euphemism
jig-jigger	Euphemism
Jim Dog	Euphemism
jimber	Noun
Jimbo	Noun
jimbrowsky	Noun
jimmy	Noun
jing-jang	Euphemism
jizz jemmy	Euphemism
jock	Noun
jockey	Noun
John	Noun
John Thomas	Euphemism
John Tom	Euphemism
Johnny Come Lately	Euphemism
Johnny Cum lately	Euphemism
Johnson	Noun

Terminology	Part of Speech
joint	Noun
Jolly Red Giant	Euphemism
jolly roger	Euphemism
jolly stick	Euphemism
joy knob	Euphemism
joy prong	Euphemism
joy stick	Euphemism
joyknob	Noun
joystick	Noun
Julius Caesar	Euphemism
kangaroo pounder	Euphemism
katana	Noun
kazoo	Noun
key	Noun
key to heaven	Euphemism
kickapoo	Noun
kickstand	Noun
kidney wiper	Euphemism
kielbasa	Noun
King Kong Dong	Euphemism
king sebastian	Euphemism
king-member	Euphemism
king's iron	Euphemism
knight	Noun
knob	Noun
knobster	Noun
krull the warrior king	Euphemism
lad	Noun
ladies' delight	Euphemism
ladies' lollipop	Euphemism
ladies' plaything	Euphemism
ladies' treasure	Euphemism
lady boner	Euphemism

Terminology	Part of Speech
Lance of love	Euphemism
lap rocket	Euphemism
Lazarus	Noun
leaky hose	Euphemism
leather cigar	Euphemism
length	Noun
lever	Noun
libido bandido	Euphemism
lingam	Noun
little Bob	Euphemism
little brother	Euphemism
Little Buddy	Euphemism
little dipper	Euphemism
little Elvis	Euphemism
little engine	Euphemism
little friend	Euphemism
little mate	Euphemism
little pinkie	Euphemism
little Ray rapin' rod	Euphemism
Little Willie	Euphemism
live wire	Euphemism
liver turner	Euphemism
lizard	Noun
loaded gun	Euphemism
lob	Noun
lob cock	Euphemism
lob prick	Euphemism
log	Noun
lollipop	Noun
long dong silver	Euphemism
long pork	Euphemism
long trade	Euphemism
longfellow	Noun

Terminology	Part of Speech
longhorn	Noun
louisville slugger	Euphemism
love bone	Euphemism
love dart	Euphemism
love gun	Euphemism
love handle	Euphemism
love hog	Euphemism
love length	Euphemism
love machine	Euphemism
love meat	Euphemism
love muscle	Euphemism
love rod	Euphemism
love sausage	Euphemism
love scepter	Euphemism
love shaft	Euphemism
love stick	Euphemism
love tool	Euphemism
love torpedo	Euphemism
love trumpet	Euphemism
love truncheon	Euphemism
love wand	Euphemism
love's battering ram	Euphemism
love's engine	Euphemism
Luigi	Noun
lung disturber	Euphemism
lust bone	Euphemism
lust shaft	Euphemism
lust sword	Euphemism
maggot	Noun
magic wand	Euphemism
magnum	Noun
main vein	Euphemism
Major Woody	Euphemism

Terminology	Part of Speech
male begetting organ	Euphemism
male interfemoral infidel	Euphemism
male intruder	Euphemism
male knout	Euphemism
male mandrel	Euphemism
male member	Euphemism
male membrum erectum	Euphemism
male monolith	Euphemism
male organ	Euphemism
male organ of generation	Euphemism
male organ of reproduction	Euphemism
male organon	Euphemism
male pendant	Euphemism
male poker	Euphemism
male pound of flesh	Euphemism
male pudendal trifler	Euphemism
male satisfier	Euphemism
male sex organ	Euphemism
male sexual organ	Euphemism
male sexual organon	Euphemism
male sinker	Euphemism
male trifler	Euphemism
male urogenital horn	Euphemism
maleness	Noun
mallet	Noun
man bone	Euphemism
man meat	Euphemism
man muscle	Euphemism
man steel	Euphemism
manbone	Noun
manhood	Noun
man-meat	Euphemism
man's best leg of three	Euphemism

Terminology	Part of Speech
man's third leg	Euphemism
marriage gear	Euphemism
masculine part	Euphemism
mast	Noun
master member	Euphemism
master of ceremonies	Euphemism
master tool	Euphemism
masterpiece	Noun
mating meat	Euphemism
mating tool	Euphemism
matrimonial peacemaker	Euphemism
mauve avenger	Euphemism
mayo shooting hot dog gun	Euphemism
maypole	Noun
meat	Noun
meat axe	Euphemism
meat cleaver	Euphemism
meat constrictor	Euphemism
meat dagger	Euphemism
meat flute	Euphemism
meat for the butcher	Euphemism
meat for the poor	Euphemism
meat popsicle	Euphemism
meat puppet	Euphemism
meat stick	Euphemism
meat thermometer	Euphemism
meat whistle	Euphemism
meat-seeking pissile	Euphemism
meatsicle	Noun
meatus longus	Euphemism
member	Noun
merrymaker	Noun
metallicrotch	Noun

Terminology	Part of Speech
meter long king kong dong	Euphemism
Mickey	Noun
microphone	Noun
middle finger	Euphemism
middle leg	Euphemism
middle stump	Euphemism
mighty meat	Euphemism
mighty sword of Eros	Euphemism
milk bone	Euphemism
milkman	Noun
missile	Noun
missile of Venus launched	Euphemism
Mister Fuzzy	Euphemism
Mister Happy	Euphemism
Mister Poky	Euphemism
Mister Softy	Euphemism
Mister Wiggly	Euphemism
modigger	Noun
Moisture and heat seeking venomous throbbing python of love	Euphemism
moisture missile	Euphemism
mole	Noun
mongoose	Noun
monster	Noun
morning wood	Euphemism
most precious part	Euphemism
mouse	Noun
Mr. Big	Euphemism
Mr. Bluevein	Euphemism
Mr. Friendly	Euphemism
Mr. Happy	Euphemism
Mr. Knish	Euphemism

Terminology	Part of Speech
Mr. Torpedo	Euphemism
Mr. Winky	Euphemism
Mr. Wong	Euphemism
muff missile	Euphemism
muscle	Noun
muscle of love	Euphemism
mushroom head	Euphemism
mutinous rogue	Euphemism
mutton bayonet	Euphemism
mutton dagger	Euphemism
mutton gun	Euphemism
mutton musket	Euphemism
my Asian buddy	Euphemism
my body's captain	Euphemism
My friend Stanley - you know, like the powerdrill	Euphemism
nail	Noun
nameless thing	Euphemism
natural member	Euphemism
nature's scythe	Euphemism
naughty toy	Euphemism
Nebraska State Capitol	Euphemism
nervous cane	Euphemism
netherrod	Noun
night stick	Euphemism
nimrod	Noun
nine iron	Euphemism
noodle	Noun
nuclear missile	Euphemism
nutrageous	Euphemism
nutty buddy	Euphemism
obelisk	Noun
octagon	Noun

Terminology	Part of Speech
Ol' One Eye	Euphemism
ol' softee	Euphemism
Old Adam	Euphemism
old Baldy	Euphemism
old blind Bob	Euphemism
old boy	Euphemism
Old Drizzly	Euphemism
Old Faithful	Euphemism
Old Faithless	Euphemism
old fella	Euphemism
old fellow	Euphemism
Old goat-peter	Euphemism
Old Hornington	Euphemism
Old Horny	Euphemism
old man	Euphemism
old warty cod	Euphemism
Omar the tentmaker	Euphemism
one-eye whale	Euphemism
one-eyed monster	Euphemism
one-eyed pants mouse	Euphemism
one-eyed trouser snake	Euphemism
one-eyed wonder weasle	Euphemism
one-eyed yogurt slinger	Euphemism
one-eyed zipper fish	Euphemism
organ	Noun
Osama bin cum'n	Euphemism
oscar	Noun
Oscar Mayer	Euphemism
P	Noun
P.D.	Euphemism
packer	Noun
pan handle	Euphemism
pant plaything	Euphemism

Terminology	Part of Speech
pantilever	Noun
pants Philistine	Euphemism
pants python	Euphemism
pants worm	Euphemism
passion pole	Euphemism
passion stick	Euphemism
patz	Noun
peacemaker	Noun
pecker	Noun
pecker wood	Euphemism
pecnoster	Noun
Pedro	Noun
pee pee	Euphemism
pee wee	Euphemism
pee-dee	Euphemism
peen	Noun
peenie	Noun
peeper	Noun
peezel	Noun
peg	Noun
pen	Noun
pen 15	Euphemism
pencil	Noun
pendulum	Noun
penis	Noun
peppermint stick	Euphemism
Perce	Noun
Percy	Noun
pet snake	Euphemism
peter	Noun
Ph. D.	Euphemism
phallating club	Euphemism
phallating stick	Euphemism

Terminology	Part of Speech
phallic clever	Euphemism
phallic pencil	Euphemism
phallic pendanta	Euphemism
phallic prod	Euphemism
phallic quencher	Euphemism
phallic scratcher	Euphemism
phallos	Noun
phallus	Noun
phallus erectus	Noun
Philly cheesesteak	Euphemism
piccolo	Noun
pickle	Noun
picklock	Noun
piddler	Noun
piece	Noun
piece of meat	Euphemism
Pied Piper	Euphemism
pig-skin bus	Euphemism
pike of pleasure	Euphemism
pike staff	Euphemism
pile driver	Euphemism
pink bus	Euphemism
pink Cadillac	Euphemism
pink oboe	Euphemism
pipe	Noun
piss handle	Euphemism
piss pipe	Euphemism
piss whistle	Euphemism
pisser	Noun
pissworm	Euphemism
pistol	Noun
piston	Noun
piston rod	Euphemism

Terminology	Part of Speech
pixie stick	Euphemism
pleasure pivot	Euphemism
plonker	Noun
plug	Noun
plunger	Noun
p-maker	Euphemism
pnor	Noun
pocket fisherman	Euphemism
pocket monster	Euphemism
pocket rocket	Euphemism
pogo-stick	Euphemism
poinswatter	Noun
point	Noun
poker	Noun
Polaroid	Noun
pole	Noun
poontanger	Noun
pop a chub	Euphemism
Popeye	Noun
popsicle	Noun
popsicle stick	Euphemism
pork sword	Euphemism
porridge gun	Euphemism
portable pocket rocket	Euphemism
potent regiment	Euphemism
prick	Noun
prickle	Noun
pride and joy	Euphemism
Prince Everhard of the Netherlands	Euphemism
private eye	Euphemism
private part	Euphemism
prod	Noun
prong	Noun

Terminology	Part of Speech
pud	Noun
pudding	Noun
pudendal intruder	Euphemism
pudendal trifler	Euphemism
pudendum	Noun
pulsing manmeat	Euphemism
pump action mottgun	Euphemism
pump handle	Euphemism
pup	Noun
puppy	Noun
Purple helmet	Euphemism
purple lollipop	Euphemism
purple-headed avenger	Euphemism
purple-headed custard chucker	Euphemism
purple-headed love truncheon	Euphemism
purple-headed meat puppet	Euphemism
purple-headed monster	Euphemism
purple-headed soldier	Euphemism
purple-headed warrior	Euphemism
purple-headed warrior man	Euphemism
purple-headed womb groom	Euphemism
purple-headed yogurt slinger	Euphemism
purple-helmeted warrior of love	Euphemism
purple-helmeted yogurt thrower	Euphemism
purple-veined tonsil tickler	Euphemism
pus rod	Euphemism
pussy diver	Euphemism
pussy feeder	Euphemism
pussy fodder	Euphemism
pussy pleaser	Euphemism
pussy plunger	Euphemism
pussy-fucker	Euphemism
pussy-poker	Euphemism

Terminology	Part of Speech
pussy-sticker	Euphemism
putter	Noun
Putz	Noun
pylon	Noun
pyramid	Noun
quickening peg	Euphemism
quiff splitter	Euphemism
quiver bone	Euphemism
rabbit	Noun
ram charger	Euphemism
ramburglar	Noun
rammer	Noun
ramrod	Noun
randy	Noun
rat	Noun
reamer	Noun
red hot poker	Euphemism
red lobster	Euphemism
remote control	Euphemism
Richard	Noun
rifle	Noun
rig	Noun
rigid digit	Euphemism
rod	Noun
rod of pleasure	Euphemism
rodger	Noun
Rodney	Noun
roger	Noun
Roger the Lodger	Euphemism
rooster	Noun
rosy red reproductive rod	Euphemism
roto-rooter	Euphemism
roundhead	Noun

Terminology	Part of Speech
rudder	Noun
ruffian	Noun
rump splitter	Euphemism
Rupert	Noun
Russell the love muscle	Euphemism
salami	Noun
salty dog	Euphemism
salty yogurt slinger	Euphemism
sausage	Noun
schlittle	Noun
schlong	Noun
schlong dongadoodle	Euphemism
schlort	Noun
schmeckle	Noun
schmuck	Noun
schnitzel	Noun
schwanz	Noun
sconge	Noun
scope	Noun
scorz	Noun
screw	Noun
screwdriver	Noun
sebastianic sword	Euphemism
Senator Packwood	Euphemism
sequoia	Noun
sex meat	Euphemism
sex stalk	Euphemism
sexing piece	Euphemism
sexocet missile	Euphemism
shaft	Noun
shmendrik	Noun
shmok	Noun
short arm	Euphemism

Terminology	Part of Speech
short leg	Euphemism
shriveller	Noun
shvantz	Noun
silky appendage	Euphemism
silver bullet	Euphemism
Sinbad	Noun
single barrelled pump-action bollock	Euphemism
skin flute	Euphemism
skinclad tube	Euphemism
slippery sex scepter	Euphemism
slug	Noun
slurpee	Noun
small arm	Euphemism
small person	Euphemism
snag	Noun
snatch pointer	Euphemism
snickers bar	Euphemism
sniper rifle	Euphemism
snotty	Noun
soldier	Noun
spam porpoise	Euphemism
spawn hammer	Euphemism
spear	Noun
sperm gun	Euphemism
spermapositor	Noun
sperminator	Noun
spike	Noun
spit	Noun
spitfire	Noun
spitter	Noun
spitting cobra	Euphemism
spooge gun	Euphemism

Terminology	Part of Speech
spout	Noun
Spunky	Noun
staff	Noun
stag	Noun
stalk	Noun
Stanley	Noun
steak	Noun
steamin' semen roadway	Euphemism
steamin' semen truck	Euphemism
steel beam	Euphemism
Steely Dan	Euphemism
stem	Noun
stick	Noun
stick shift	Euphemism
sticker	Noun
stickshift	Noun
sticky finger	Euphemism
sticky grenade	Euphemism
sticky spud gun	Euphemism
stiff	Noun
stiffy	Noun
stinger	Noun
stocking stuffer	Euphemism
stout warrior	Euphemism
strap	Noun
straw	Noun
stretcher	Noun
stud	Noun
stud meat	Noun
Stumpy	Noun
sugar stick	Euphemism
superdick	Noun
surf board	Euphemism

Terminology	Part of Speech
swartz	Noun
sweet meat	Euphemism
swizzle stick	Euphemism
sword	Noun
tail	Noun
tail-line	Noun
tallywhacker	Noun
tan banana	Euphemism
tan trouser snake	Euphemism
tarzoon	Noun
tassle	Noun
tent peg	Euphemism
Texas longhorn	Euphemism
the assault rifle	Euphemism
the battleship	Euphemism
the big fella	Euphemism
the colonel	Euphemism
The Eighth Wonder of the World	Euphemism
the goods	Euphemism
the grenade	Euphemism
the key	Euphemism
the lad	Euphemism
the land mine	Euphemism
the lawnmower	Euphemism
The lieutenant	Euphemism
the lightsaber	Euphemism
The Lincoln Memorial	Euphemism
the machete	Euphemism
the machine	Euphemism
the major	Euphemism
the mustang	Euphemism
the pendulum	Euphemism
the punisher	Euphemism

Terminology	Part of Speech
the purple beret	Euphemism
the seaman	Euphemism
The sixth Beatle	Euphemism
The Titanic	Euphemism
the useless	Euphemism
The Washington Monument	Euphemism
the water gun	Euphemism
the worm	Euphemism
thingie	Noun
thingy	Noun
third leg	Euphemism
three card trick	Euphemism
throat spackler	Euphemism
throb knob	Euphemism
throbber	Noun
throbbing giggle stick	Euphemism
throbbing manliness	Euphemism
thumb	Noun
thumb of love	Euphemism
thunderbird 3	Euphemism
thundersword	Noun
tinker	Noun
todger	Noun
Tom Thumb	Euphemism
tom-tom	Euphemism
tong	Noun
tonk	Noun
tonsil tickler	Euphemism
tonsil wrench	Euphemism
toobsnake	Euphemism
toobsteak	Euphemism
tool	Noun
tool of pleasure	Euphemism

Terminology	Part of Speech
toot meat	Euphemism
Top Gun	Euphemism
torch of Cupid	Euphemism
torpedo	Noun
tossergash	Noun
towel rack	Euphemism
toy	Noun
toy soldier	Euphemism
tramp killer	Euphemism
tree of life	Euphemism
tree of love	Euphemism
Tricky Dick	Euphemism
trifle	Noun
trigger	Noun
tripod	Noun
trombone	Noun
trouser ferret	Euphemism
trouser mauser	Euphemism
trouser snake	Euphemism
trouser toy	Euphemism
trouser trick	Euphemism
trouser trout	Euphemism
trouser trumpet	Euphemism
trouser truncheon	Euphemism
trouser worm	Euphemism
trumpet	Noun
tube of meat	Euphemism
tube snake	Euphemism
tube steak	Euphemism
tug muscle	Euphemism
tummy banana	Euphemism
tummy tickler	Euphemism
turkey baster	Euphemism

Terminology	Part of Speech
turtle head	Euphemism
twanger	Noun
tweeterfrank	Noun
twig	Noun
twinkie	Noun
Twix	Noun
ugly little dog Dick	Euphemism
uncle	Noun
Uncle Dick	Euphemism
undercover brother	Euphemism
underpant eel	Euphemism
unit	Noun
upright grand	Euphemism
urinary pet cock	Euphemism
urogenital tailpiece	Euphemism
vaginal dilator	Euphemism
vegetable stick	Euphemism
vein	Noun
vein laden meat pipe	Euphemism
veiny bang stick	Euphemism
veiny salami	Euphemism
verge	Noun
VIP	Euphemism
virgin's dream	Euphemism
virile member	Euphemism
vitals	Noun
vomer	Noun
voorsch	Noun
wacker	Noun
wad	Noun
wag	Noun
walking tripod	Euphemism
Waltzin' Downstairs Matilda	Euphemism

Terminology	Part of Speech
wammer	Noun
wand	Noun
wang	Noun
wang bone	Euphemism
wang doodle	Euphemism
wang stick	Euphemism
wangdoodle	Noun
wanger	Noun
wang-tang	Euphemism
wank rod	Euphemism
wanker	Noun
warhammer	Noun
warm member	Euphemism
water pistol	Euphemism
wazzock	Noun
weapon	Noun
wedding kit	Euphemism
wedge bone	Euphemism
wee	Noun
wee wee	Euphemism
weiner	Noun
weiner schnitzle	Euphemism
weinie	Noun
whacker	Noun
whalebone	Noun
whammer	Noun
whang	Noun
whangdoodle	Noun
whanger	Noun
whanker	Noun
whatsus	Noun
whip	Noun
whip whistle	Euphemism

Terminology	Part of Speech
whisker splitter	Euphemism
whiskey dick	Euphemism
whistle	Noun
who who dilly	Euphemism
whoopie stick	Euphemism
whopper	Noun
wick	Noun
Wicked Willie	Euphemism
wife's best friend	Euphemism
wigga-wagga	Euphemism
willie	Noun
Willy the burping worm	Euphemism
wing dang doodle	Euphemism
wingdoodle	Noun
winky	Noun
winny popper	Euphemism
wire	Noun
wishbone	Noun
WMD	Euphemism
woman pleaser	Euphemism
womb broom	Euphemism
womb bruiser	Euphemism
womb brush	Euphemism
womb cannon	Euphemism
womb ferret	Euphemism
won ton	Euphemism
wong	Noun
wonger	Noun
Wood	Noun
Woodrow	Noun
Woody Johnson	Euphemism
woofer	Noun
wooter	Noun

Terminology	Part of Speech
wop	Noun
worm	Noun
worm with a nazi helmet	Euphemism
wriggling pole	Euphemism
wriggling stick	Euphemism
wurst	Noun
yack	Noun
yang	Noun
yang fella	Euphemism
yard	Noun
yardage	Noun
yards of personality	Euphemism
ying yang	Euphemism
ying-yang	Euphemism
yogurt gun	Euphemism
yogurt shotgun	Euphemism
yoo hoo	Euphemism
yoyo	Noun
yutz	Noun
zab	Noun
Zeus	Noun
zipperfish	Noun
zoob	Noun
zoobrick	Noun
zubb	Noun
zubra	Noun
zubrick	Noun
zuchini	Noun

Penis and Testicles

Terminology	Part of Speech
auxiliaries	Noun
balls and bat	Euphemism
Big Dick and the twins	Euphemism
Big Jim and the twins	Euphemism
billy and doo	Euphemism
boss and his two helpers	Euphemism
dong and gongs	Euphemism
gear and tool	Euphemism
general, two colonels	Euphemism
ham and two eggs	Euphemism
meat and two potatoes	Euphemism
okra and prunes	Euphemism
string and nuggets	Euphemism
twig and berries	Euphemism
two balls and a whistle	Euphemism
Uncle Jim and the twins	Euphemism

Perineum

Terminology	Part of Speech
chode	Noun
barse	Noun
nifkin	Noun
taint	Noun

Pubic Hair

Terminology	Part of Speech
belly bristles	Euphemism
belly thicket	Euphemism
cluster	Noun
curlies	Noun
curls	Noun
curly hairs	Noun
dick wheat	Euphemism
gorilla salad	Euphemism
pubes	Noun
short and curlies	Euphemism
short hairs	Euphemism

Pubic Hairs and Genitals

Terminology	Part of Speech
hairy escutcheon	Euphemism

Scrotum

Terminology	Part of Speech
bag	Noun
bag of fruits	Euphemism
ball bag	Euphemism
ball basket	Euphemism
ball holder	Euphemism
ballock bag	Euphemism
bawbag	Noun
bean bag	Euphemism
bollock bag	Euphemism
bollock-bag	Euphemism
bozack	Noun
chin knocker	Euphemism
coin purse	Euphemism
cookies	Noun
cowbell	Noun
daddy bag	Euphemism
Deez Nutz	Euphemism
fruit bowl	Euphemism
grand bag	Euphemism
guy sack	Euphemism
hairy beanbag	Euphemism
hairy saddlebags	Euphemism
hanging pleasure	Euphemism
happy sack	Euphemism
jelly bag	Euphemism
jewel box	Euphemism

Terminology	Part of Speech
jiblets	Noun
jizz bag	Euphemism
jizzbags	Noun
junk	Noun
knapsack	Noun
knob sack	Euphemism
lamel	Noun
little men	Euphemism
love custard	Euphemism
male pouch	Euphemism
marble sack	Euphemism
my boys	Euphemism
nad bag	Euphemism
nad sack	Euphemism
noogies	Noun
nut bag	Euphemism
package	Noun
plucked turkey	Euphemism
pouch	Noun
protein pendulum	Euphemism
purse	Noun
raisin bag	Euphemism
sack	Noun
sack of salt	Euphemism
scrot	Noun
scrot-num	Euphemism
scrot-sack	Euphemism
scruffies	Noun
sleeping bag	Euphemism
sperm sack	Euphemism
tadpole carrier	Euphemism
tea bag	Euphemism
tomb of the precious jewels	Euphemism

Terminology	Part of Speech
tool bag	Euphemism
under the butt nut hut	Euphemism
wad	Noun
wally	Noun
winky bag	Euphemism
yam bag	Euphemism
zack	Noun

Semen

Terminology	Part of Speech
albino custard	Euphemism
Aphrodites Evostick	Euphemism
arse grease	Euphemism
ass grease	Euphemism
axle grease	Euphemism
baby custard	Euphemism
baby fat	Euphemism
baby food	Euphemism
baby gravy	Euphemism
baby juice	Euphemism
baby paste	Euphemism
baby's	Euphemism
ball-bearing oil	Euphemism
baume de vie	Euphemism
beef extract	Euphemism
beef gravy	Euphemism
belly seed	Euphemism
boy honey	Euphemism
bull gravy	Euphemism
bullets	Noun
bung juice	Euphemism

Terminology	Part of Speech
bung spew	Euphemism
butter	Noun
buttermilk	Noun
chism	Noun
chitty	Noun
cock paste	Euphemism
cock porridge	Euphemism
cock puke	Euphemism
cock snot	Euphemism
cock vomit	Euphemism
cock wax	Euphemism
cocoa butter	Euphemism
come	Noun
come juice	Euphemism
comings	Noun
courting cream	Euphemism
cream	Noun
cream sauce	Euphemism
crud	Noun
crunt	Noun
cum	Noun
cum cum	Euphemism
cundy	Noun
Cupid's toothpaste	Euphemism
curd	Noun
custard	Noun
Cyclop's tears	Euphemism
daddy's sauce	Euphemism
dew on the lily	Euphemism
dick butter	Euphemism
dick drink	Euphemism
dicksplash	Noun
discharge	Noun

Terminology	Part of Speech
dog water	Euphemism
doll spit	Euphemism
dream whip	Euphemism
ejaculant	Noun
emission	Noun
emok	Noun
face cream	Euphemism
father stuff	Euphemism
fetch	Noun
foam	Noun
French dressing	Euphemism
French-fried ice cream	Euphemism
French-fried ice water	Euphemism
froth	Noun
fruit juice	Euphemism
fuck	Noun
gentleman's relish	Euphemism
germen	Noun
germin	Noun
gism	Noun
gissom	Noun
gisum	Noun
gizzum	Noun
glaze	Noun
glop	Noun
gloy	Noun
glue	Noun
goat's milk	Euphemism
gonad glue	Euphemism
goo	Noun
googoo	Noun
gravy	Noun
gub	Noun

Terminology	Part of Speech
gubb	Noun
hand lotion	Euphemism
happy juice	Euphemism
herbalz	Noun
hockey	Noun
home brew	Euphemism
honey	Noun
hookey	Noun
hooky	Noun
hot fat	Euphemism
hot juice	Euphemism
hot lead	Euphemism
hot milk	Euphemism
Irish confetti	Euphemism
jack	Noun
jam	Noun
jazz	Noun
jelly	Noun
jelly juice	Euphemism
jerk jelly	Euphemism
jerk juice	Euphemism
jessom	Noun
jet stream	Euphemism
jip	Noun
jis	Noun
jisem	Noun
jism	Noun
jissom	Noun
jiz	Noun
jizz	Noun
jizzom	Noun
jizzum	Noun
joombye	Noun

Terminology	Part of Speech
joy juice	Euphemism
juice	Noun
junk	Noun
krud	Noun
lather	Noun
lewd infusion	Euphemism
liquid hair dressing	Euphemism
load	Noun
love butter	Euphemism
love custard	Euphemism
love juice	Euphemism
love liquid	Euphemism
love liquor	Euphemism
love's nectar	Euphemism
lumpy piss	Euphemism
man chowder	Euphemism
man juice	Euphemism
man milk	Euphemism
man mustard	Euphemism
man oil	Euphemism
man soup	Euphemism
manfat	Noun
manglaze	Noun
manglue	Noun
man's milk	Euphemism
maria	Noun
marrow	Noun
marrow pudding	Euphemism
mayonaise	Noun
McSpunk	Noun
mecotero	Noun
melted butter	Euphemism
mess	Noun

Terminology	Part of Speech
mettle	Noun
mettle of generation	Euphemism
milk	Noun
milt	Noun
minkus	Noun
muck	Noun
muckle	Noun
mungle	Noun
oil of man	Euphemism
ointment	Noun
oyster	Noun
paste	Noun
pearl	Noun
pearl drop	Euphemism
pearly passion juice	Euphemism
pecker snot	Euphemism
pedigree chum	Euphemism
people paste	Euphemism
phallic ejaculant	Euphemism
phallic vomitus	Euphemism
pineapple chunk	Euphemism
pod juice	Euphemism
population paste	Euphemism
pre-cum	Noun
prick juice	Euphemism
protein	Noun
pudding	Noun
queen bees	Euphemism
Reproductive fluid	Noun
rice pudding	Euphemism
rich cream sauce	Euphemism
roe	Noun
royal jelly	Euphemism

Terminology	Part of Speech
sauce	Noun
scum	Noun
seed	Noun
seminal discharge	Noun
seminal fluid	Noun
seminal milk	Euphemism
sexual discharge	Euphemism
sexual spendings	Euphemism
shissom	Noun
slime	Noun
slizz	Noun
smud	Noun
snake venom	Euphemism
snedge	Noun
snot	Noun
snowstorm	Noun
soap	Noun
soul sauce	Euphemism
Spanish rice	Euphemism
spence	Noun
spend	Noun
spendlings	Noun
sperm	Noun
spermatic juice	Euphemism
spew	Noun
splash	Noun
splooch	Noun
splooge	Noun
sponge	Noun
spoo	Noun
spooch	Noun
spooey	Noun
spoof	Noun

Terminology	Part of Speech
spoonta	Noun
spratz	Noun
spudwater	Noun
spuff	Noun
spume	Noun
spunk	Noun
spunk	Noun
starch	Noun
stick	Noun
stick it	Euphemism
sticky	Euphemism
sticky seed	Euphemism
stitch	Noun
stuff	Noun
suds	Noun
tadpole treasure	Euphemism
tail juice	Euphemism
tail oil	Euphemism
tail water	Euphemism
tapioca pudding	Euphemism
tapioca toothpaste	Euphemism
turnip seeds	Euphemism
vitamins	Noun
wad	Noun
water of life	Euphemism
wazz	Noun
whipped cream	Euphemism
white blow	Euphemism
white honey	Euphemism
white love piss	Euphemism
white swallow	Euphemism
whitewash	Noun
whore's milk	Euphemism

Terminology	Part of Speech
yogurt	Noun
yuk	Noun

Testicles

Terminology	Part of Speech
acorn	Noun
acorns	Noun
allsbay	Noun
apples	Noun
apricots	Noun
baby makers	Euphemism
back wheels	Euphemism
ball	Noun
balls	Noun
bangers	Noun
bangles	Noun
bannocks	Noun
baubles	Noun
bean pods	Euphemism
Beavis and Butthead	Euphemism
bells	Noun
billiards	Noun
bird eggs	Euphemism
bird's eggs	Euphemism
bojangles	Noun
bollock	Noun
bollocks	Noun
bonbons	Noun
booboos	Noun
boys	Noun
bubus	Noun

Terminology	Part of Speech
bullets	Noun
bum balls	Euphemism
bum-balls	Euphemism
Charleys	Noun
cherry	Noun
chestnuts	Noun
chicken Mc Nuggets	Euphemism
chicken McNuggets	Euphemism
chones	Noun
Christmas crackers	Euphemism
chuckies	Noun
clappers	Noun
cobbles	Noun
cobbs	Noun
cobs	Noun
cockles	Noun
coconuts	Noun
cojones	Noun
come factories	Euphemism
coolies	Noun
cream donuts	Euphemism
cullions	Noun
culls	Noun
damsons	Noun
dangly bits	Euphemism
diamonds	Noun
ding-dangs	Euphemism
ding-dongs	Euphemism
dojiggers	Noun
doo dahs	Euphemism
dumbbells	Noun
dusters	Noun
Easter eggs	Euphemism

Terminology	Part of Speech
eggs	Noun
eggs in a basket	Euphemism
family jewels	Euphemism
fiery coals	Euphemism
figs	Noun
flack	Noun
flowers and frolics	Euphemism
frick	Noun
frick and frack	Euphemism
fun and frolics	Euphemism
gadgets	Noun
gear	Noun
General smuts	Euphemism
giggle berries	Euphemism
glands	Noun
globes	Noun
goatees	Noun
gonads	Noun
gones	Noun
gongs	Noun
gonicles	Noun
goolies	Noun
grapes	Noun
grenades	Noun
groin	Noun
hairy conkers	Euphemism
hangers	Noun
heirlooms	Noun
huevos	Noun
itchy and scratchy	Euphemism
Jackson Pollocks	Euphemism
jelly beans	Euphemism
jingle bells	Euphemism

Terminology	Part of Speech
Johnny Rollicks	Euphemism
Johnny Rollocks	Euphemism
jumbucks	Noun
kaks	Noun
kelks	Noun
kiwi	Noun
knackers	Noun
knacks	Noun
little acorns	Euphemism
Little Buddy's buddies	Euphemism
love apples	Euphemism
love nuts	Euphemism
love spuds	Euphemism
low hangers	Euphemism
low-hangers	Euphemism
maracas	Noun
marbles	Noun
marshmallows	Noun
meatballs	Noun
meaty bites	Euphemism
meggs	Noun
nackers	Noun
nadds	Noun
nadgers	Noun
nads	Noun
nard	Noun
nards	Noun
norks	Noun
nuggets	Noun
nutmegs	Noun
nuts	Noun
orbs	Noun
orchids	Noun

Terminology	Part of Speech
ornaments	Noun
package	Noun
peanuts	Noun
plum	Noun
plums	Noun
pounders	Noun
prairie oysters	Euphemism
prunes	Noun
Reece's Pieces	Euphemism
rocks	Noun
rollies	Noun
rollocks	Noun
sandbags	Noun
Sandra Bullocks	Euphemism
scalloped potatoes	Euphemism
scallops	Noun
seals	Noun
sex slabs	Euphemism
slabs	Noun
slappers	Noun
spunk bunkers	Euphemism
spunk factories	Euphemism
spunk holders	Euphemism
stones	Noun
swamp nuts	Euphemism
sweetbread	Noun
sweets	Noun
swingers	Noun
tarn-wags	Euphemism
tarry wags	Euphemism
taters	Noun
tatties	Noun
testacolas	Noun

Terminology	Part of Speech
testes	Noun
testimonials	Noun
testosities	Noun
testostities	Noun
test-ticklers	Euphemism
The Balkans	Euphemism
the sperm factory	Euphemism
The Twins	Euphemism
the two amigos	Euphemism
The Urals	Euphemism
thingamabobs	Noun
thingamajigs	Noun
thingummies	Noun
truffles	Noun
Tweedledee and Tweedledum	Euphemism
twiddle-diddles	Euphemism
velvet orbs	Euphemism
walnuts	Noun
wank tanks	Euphemism
water balloons	Euphemism
wedding tackle	Euphemism
wheels	Noun
yarbles	Noun
yongles	Noun

Tongue

Terminology	Part of Speech
clack	Noun
clacker	Noun
clapper	Noun

3. SEXUAL ACTS

Anal Sex Either

Terminology	Part of Speech
66	Euphemism
99	Euphemism
a bit of brown	Euphemism
a bit of ring	Euphemism
a-bucking	Verb
ace fuck	Euphemism
anal coitus	Noun
anal dance	Euphemism
anal delight	Euphemism
anal job	Noun
analize	Euphemism
anogenital intercourse	Noun
ass-fuck	Euphemism
ass-fucking	Verb
B.F.	Euphemism
back jump	Euphemism
back-door boogie	Euphemism
back-door work	Euphemism
backgammon	Euphemism
back-gammon	Euphemism
baloney calonic	Euphemism
banging fudge	Euphemism
base fuck	Euphemism
batter the sausage	Euphemism
behind door work	Euphemism
behind the behind	Euphemism
bend some ham	Euphemism
bend someone over	Euphemism
BF	Euphemism

Terminology	Part of Speech
bit of brown	Euphemism
bit of ring	Euphemism
bit of tail	Euphemism
bone in the bum	Euphemism
bone the bum	Euphemism
boogie	Verb
boom-boom	Euphemism
bore	Verb
boring bud	Euphemism
boring a bud	Verb
bot	Verb
bottom's up	Euphemism
broaden someone's outlook	Euphemism
broom	Euphemism
broom-in-the-cave	Euphemism
brown eye	Euphemism
brown hole	Euphemism
browning	Verb
bubble	Verb
bufu	Noun
bugger	Verb
buggering	Verb
buggery	Noun
bum fuck	Noun
bum fucking	Verb
bumholerous fuckerous	Euphemism
bumming	Verb
burgle	Verb
bury one's ring	Euphemism
butt balling	Verb
butt bang	Noun
butt banging	Verb
butt fuck	Noun

Terminology	Part of Speech
butt fucking	Verb
butt in	Verb
butt play	Noun
butthole surfing	Euphemism
buttplay	Verb
chocolate cha cha	Euphemism
chocolate speedway	Euphemism
code brown	Euphemism
coitus in anum	Euphemism
coitus in anus	Euphemism
coitus in rectum	Euphemism
coitus per anum	Euphemism
coitus per rectum	Euphemism
cornholing	Verb
crap hole fuck	Euphemism
cruising the hershey highway	Euphemism
delivering to dirtbox drive	Euphemism
dinner mashing	Euphemism
dip in the fudge pot	Euphemism
dirt road racing	Euphemism
do a stern job	Euphemism
dog fuck	Euphemism
dog in the bathtub	Euphemism
drilling for marmite	Euphemism
drive it up to Hilltop Drive	Euphemism
Enjoy a stroll down Cadbury alley	Euphemism
Enjoy a stroll down Cadbury Avenue	Euphemism
Enjoy a stroll down Cadbury Canal	Euphemism
file in the wrong box	Euphemism
fishing for brown trout	Euphemism
fluff the duff	Euphemism
foop	Euphemism

Terminology	Part of Speech
fuck buttock	Euphemism
fuck in the ass	Euphemism
fudge packing	Euphemism
get some brown sugar	Euphemism
get some mud for the duck	Euphemism
get some round eye	Euphemism
go Hollywood	Euphemism
go up the dirt road	Euphemism
going down the dirt road	Euphemism
going down the Hershey highway	Euphemism
going up the ass	Euphemism
going up the chute	Euphemism
going up the Hershey bar road	Euphemism
going up the mustard road	Euphemism
going up the old dirt road	Euphemism
Gr	Euphemism
Gr act	Euphemism
Greek	Noun
Greek fashion	Euphemism
Greek love	Euphemism
Greek style	Euphemism
Greek way	Euphemism
greeking	Euphemism
gut-reaming	Euphemism
have a bit of bum	Euphemism
have a bit of tail	Euphemism
high-Greek	Euphemism
hot-dogging	Verb
in the brown	Euphemism
intercourse per anum	Euphemism
in-the-brown	Euphemism
keester stab	Euphemism
kicking the backdoor in	Verb

Terminology	Part of Speech
kiester stab	Euphemism
mix your peanut butter	Euphemism
molly	Verb
moon shot	Euphemism
open up someone's ass	Euphemism
open up the ass	Euphemism
pack fudge	Euphemism
pack some fudge	Euphemism
packin' mud	Verb
packing fudge	Verb
packing mud	Verb
part cheeks	Euphemism
part someone's cheeks	Euphemism
penoanal intercourse	Euphemism
phallate per rectum	Euphemism
pipe	Verb
play checkers	Euphemism
play dump truck	Euphemism
play leapfrog	Euphemism
pot of brown	Euphemism
Pound	Verb
pound someone's ass	Verb
pound the ass	Verb
pound the butt	Verb
pound the cheeks	Verb
punk	Verb
ram job	Euphemism
ram the dam	Verb
rear entry	Euphemism
ride up the dirt road	Euphemism
rocky roading	Verb
RR 3	Euphemism
rump work	Euphemism

Terminology	Part of Speech
Rural Route 3	Euphemism
sail into the wind	Euphemism
screw some ass	Verb
shaft in the bum	Euphemism
shit fuck	Euphemism
shit stabbing	Verb
shoot at the back door	Verb
shoot in the back	Verb
shoot in the brown	Verb
shoot in the tail	Verb
shoot the star	Verb
shoot up the straight	Verb
shortcake	Euphemism
shot at the back door	Verb
Sin of Sodom	Noun
sink the brown	Euphemism
sitting on it	Verb
sixty-six	Euphemism
slate bowl	Euphemism
slate plate	Euphemism
slick and slim up the old dusty road	Euphemism
snag	Verb
sod	Verb
sodomize	Verb
sodomy	Noun
sotadism	Noun
split some buns	Verb
split someone's buns	Verb
stern approach	Euphemism
stern job	Euphemism
stir a little fudge	Verb
stir chocolate	Verb
stir fudge	Verb

Terminology	Part of Speech
stir shit	Verb
stir some shit	Verb
stir someone's chocolate	Verb
stir someone's fudge	Verb
stir someone's shit	Verb
stretch some jeans	Verb
tail job	Euphemism
take a trip to the moon	Euphemism
take the Hershey highway	Euphemism
third way	Euphemism
throw a button hole on	Euphemism
trip to the moon	Euphemism
turn over	Euphemism
turnover	Euphemism
unmentionable vice	Euphemism
unnatural connection	Euphemism
unnatural debauchery	Euphemism
unnatural sexual intercourse	Euphemism
unnatural vice	Euphemism
up bosco boulevard	Euphemism
up the ass	Euphemism
up the bosco boulevard	Euphemism
up the brown	Euphemism
up the bum	Euphemism
up the butt	Euphemism
up the chocolate highway	Euphemism
up the dirt road	Euphemism
up the mustard road	Euphemism
up the old dirt road	Euphemism
up the shitter	Euphemism
up the ying-yang	Euphemism
uts	Euphemism
vice allemand	Euphemism

Terminology	Part of Speech
wall job	Euphemism
worship at the back altar	Euphemism
wreck a rectum	Euphemism
zorber	Verb

Anal Sex Female

Terminology	Part of Speech
bottle	Verb

Anal Sex Male

Terminology	Part of Speech
bung	Verb
bunghole	Verb
bung-hole	Verb
dot the I	Euphemism
plug	Verb
reamer	Noun
sailor's cup of tea	Euphemism
tunnel	Verb

Anal Sex Male Point of View

Terminology	Part of Speech
bury the bone in the backyard	Euphemism
popping it in the toaster	Verb

Anal Sex Face to Face

Terminology	Part of Speech
a-buck	Noun

Anal Masturbation Either

Terminology	Part of Speech
finger fuck	Euphemism
finger job	Euphemism
postillionage	Noun

Deflower a Female Virgin

Terminology	Part of Speech
axed	Verb
battered	Verb
be the first	Euphemism
blaze the trail	Euphemism
break a crust	Euphemism
break a leg	Euphemism
break her	Euphemism
break her hymen	Euphemism
break her leg above the knee	Euphemism
broach claret	Euphemism
broke her teacup	Euphemism
broken	Adjective

Terminology	Part of Speech
broken-kneed	Euphemism
broken-legged	Euphemism
bust cherry	Euphemism
cherry harvest	Euphemism
cherry pick	Euphemism
cherrypop	Euphemism
chop-chop	Euphemism
clipped in the ring	Euphemism
cocked	Verb
to break	Euphemism

Deflower a Male Virgin

Terminology	Part of Speech
break in the balls	Euphemism
break open the pie	Verb
crack a teacup	Euphemism
papa cherry	Euphemism
pluck-a-rose	Verb
pop a cherry	Euphemism
poppa-cherry	Euphemism

Female Masturbation

Terminology	Part of Speech
a little southern romance	Euphemism
accordion solo	Euphemism
airing the orchid	Euphemism
applying lip gloss	Euphemism
auditioning the finger puppet	Euphemism
basting the meat	Euphemism
basting the tuna	Euphemism

Terminology	Part of Speech
be you own best friend	Euphemism
beat the beaver	Euphemism
beating about the bush	Euphemism
beating around the bush	Euphemism
beating the bush	Euphemism
bisecting the triangle	Euphemism
blooming	Verb
bouginonia	Verb
bring oneself off	Euphemism
bringing oneself off	Euphemism
brushing the beaver	Euphemism
buff the beaver	Euphemism
buff the weasel	Euphemism
buffing the box	Euphemism
buffing the jewel	Euphemism
bury the knuckle	Euphemism
butter schlopping	Euphemism
butter the head	Euphemism
butter the muffin	Euphemism
butter the potato	Euphemism
butting the bead	Euphemism
buttonhole	Verb
buying an E-ticket	Euphemism
buzz	Verb
buzzing	Verb
candle sticking	Verb
caning the vandal	Euphemism
caress oneself	Euphemism
caressing the kitty	Euphemism
checking the foxhole	Euphemism
checking the status of the I/O port	Euphemism
churning the cream	Euphemism
circling the knoll	Euphemism

Terminology	Part of Speech
clam bake for one	Euphemism
clap the clit	Euphemism
clap with one hand	Euphemism
cleaning my fur coat	Euphemism
cleaning the fingers	Euphemism
cleaning the fish	Euphemism
cleaning your fingers	Euphemism
clit bliss	Euphemism
clit fix	Euphemism
clit twit	Euphemism
clubbing the clam	Euphemism
do the bowling hold	Verb
finger fuck	Euphemism
finger job	Euphemism
fingerdoodling	Verb
frig	Verb
going blind	Verb
play stink-finger	Euphemism
play stinky-pinky	Euphemism
press the button	Euphemism
six pack	Verb
stink anger	Euphemism
stinky-pinky	Euphemism
taking care of business	Euphemism

Female Masturbation with Large Items

Terminology	Part of Speech
brachioproctic eroticism	Noun
brachiovaginal eroticism	Noun

Female Virgin Sex

Terminology	Part of Speech
axed	Euphemism
be the first	Euphemism
blaze the trail	Euphemism
break a cherry	Euphemism
break a crust	Euphemism
break a leg	Euphemism
break her	Euphemism
break her hymen	Euphemism
break her leg above the knee	Euphemism
break open the pi	Euphemism
broach claret	Euphemism
broke her teacutp	Euphemism
broken	Adjective
broken-kneed	Euphemism
broken-legged	Euphemism
bust cherry	Euphemism
cherry harvest	Euphemism
cherry pick	Euphemism
cherrypop	Euphemism
chop-chop	Euphemism
clipped in the ring	Euphemism
cocked	Verb
crack a teacup	Euphemism
papa cherry	Euphemism
pluck-a-rose	Verb
pop a cherry	Euphemism
poppa-cherry	Euphemism
to break	Euphemism
battered	Adjective

Foreplay

Terminology	Part of Speech
canoodling	Verb
caressing	Verb
contrectation	Noun
erotic congress	Euphemism
fondling	Verb
fool around (with)	Euphemism
fooling around	Verb
fore-pleasure	Noun
grab ass	Euphemism
horse around	Verb
jack around	Verb
jazz around	Verb
knick-knacking	Verb
lovins	Noun
make nice	Euphemism
make out	Euphemism
making out	Verb
mess about	Euphemism
mess around	Euphemism
nick-nacking	Verb
night baseball	Euphemism
night exercise	Euphemism
night games	Euphemism
nookey-push-push	Euphemism
nooky-push-push	Euphemism
old slap and tickle	Euphemism
petting	Verb
play around (with)	Euphemism
play at pickle-me-tickle-me	Euphemism
play pickle-me-tickle-me	Euphemism
play snuggle bunnies	Euphemism
slap 'n tickle	Euphemism

Terminology	Part of Speech
slap-and-tickle	Euphemism
smooching	Verb
warm up	Euphemism

French Kiss

Terminology	Part of Speech
box tonsils	Euphemism
deep kissing	Euphemism
mouth wrestling	Euphemism
pass secrets	Euphemism
soul kissing	Euphemism
suck face	Euphemism
swab the tonsils	Euphemism
throw the tongue	Euphemism
tongue kissing	Euphemism
tongue sushi	Euphemism
tongue wrestling	Euphemism
wet kissing	Euphemism

Genital Sex - Either

Terminology	Part of
a bit of bouncy-bouncy	Euphemism
a bit of cuddle	Euphemism
a bit of front door work	Euphemism
a bit of fun	Euphemism
a bit of hard for a bit of soft	Euphemism
a bit of it	Euphemism
a bit of nobble	Euphemism
a bit of nookey	Euphemism
a bit of nookie	Euphemism

Terminology	Part of
a bit of nooky	Euphemism
a bit of raspberry	Euphemism
a bit of rumpty-tumpty	Euphemism
a bit of rumpy-bumpy	Euphemism
a bit of rumpy-pumpy	Euphemism
a bit of sex	Euphemism
a bit of skin	Euphemism
a bit of snug	Euphemism
a bit of stiff	Euphemism
a bit of the other	Euphemism
a little one-on-one	Euphemism
a piece of flesh	Euphemism
a spot of hard breathing	Euphemism
a spot of heavy breathing	Euphemism
aardvark	Euphemism
act of androgynation	Euphemism
act of love	Euphemism
act of pleasure	Euphemism
Adam-and-Eve-it	Euphemism
afternoon delight	Euphemism
afternooner	Euphemism
all the way	Euphemism
at it	Euphemism
baby-making love	Euphemism
bad thing	Euphemism
bag	Verb
bam bam	Euphemism
bananas and cream	Euphemism
bandicooting	Verb
bang	Verb
bang away	Euphemism
bang like a shit house door	Euphemism
bang like a shit house door in a gale	Euphemism

Terminology	Part of
bang like a shit house door in the wind	Euphemism
banging	Verb
BBQ'N	Verb
be intimate with	Euphemism
beanfest	Euphemism
bear play	Euphemism
beast with two backs	Euphemism
bed	Verb
bed down	Euphemism
bed down with	Euphemism
bed someone	Euphemism
bedtime story	Euphemism
bedventure	Euphemism
bedwork	Euphemism
belly ride	Euphemism
belly slapping	Euphemism
belly warmer	Euphemism
belly-bump	Euphemism
belly-bumping	Euphemism
bellying	Verb
belly-to-belly	Adjective
big number	Euphemism
big time	Euphemism
biological event	Euphemism
bit of beef	Euphemism
bit of bouncy bouncy	Euphemism
bit of butt	Euphemism
bit of cuddle	Euphemism
bit of fat	Euphemism
bit of fat	Euphemism
bit of meat	Euphemism
bit of nifty	Euphemism

Terminology	Part of
bit of nobble	Euphemism
bit of nookie	Euphemism
bit of nooky	Euphemism
bit of rumpty-tumpty	Euphemism
bit of rumpy-bumpy	Euphemism
bit of rumpy-pumpy	Euphemism
bit of skin	Euphemism
bit of snug	Euphemism
bit of stiff	Euphemism
bit of stuff	Euphemism
bit of tail	Euphemism
bit of the other	Euphemism
bit on the fork	Euphemism
biz	Noun
blow off loose corns	Euphemism
bob	Verb
boff	Verb
boffing	Verb
boink	Verb
boinking	Verb
bone dance	Euphemism
bone up	Euphemism
boning	Verb
bonk	Noun
boogie	Verb
boom-boom	Euphemism
booty	Noun
booty-call	Euphemism
bop	Verb
bounce in bed	Euphemism
bouncy-bouncy	Euphemism
box	Verb
box the compass	Euphemism

Terminology	Part of
breakfast nook	Euphemism
breed	Verb
brim	Verb
buck	Verb
buckwilding	Verb
bull session	Noun
bulling	Verb
bump and grind	Euphemism
bump bellies	Euphemism
bump bones	Euphemism
bump nasties	Euphemism
bump pelvis	Euphemism
bump uglies	Euphemism
bumping uglies	Euphemism
bury face upwards	Euphemism
butter and eggs	Euphemism
candy	Noun
cap	Verb
carnal acquaintance	Euphemism
carnal connection	Euphemism
carnal engagement	Euphemism
carnal knowledge	Euphemism
carnal pleasures	Euphemism
carnival knowledge	Euphemism
carry-me-down	Euphemism
chafer	Verb
chunk	Euphemism
coitus	Verb
copulate	Verb
cush	Verb
cut	Verb
do the bad thing	Euphemism
do the nasty	Euphemism

Terminology	Part of
do the naughty	Euphemism
do the you-know-what	Euphemism
drive	Verb
futz	Verb
F-word	Euphemism
gasp and grunt	Euphemism
get buckwild	Euphemism
give someone the business	Euphemism
go the whole way	Euphemism
grasp and grunt	Euphemism
groan and grunt	Euphemism
growl and grunt	Euphemism
grumble and grunt	Euphemism
jazz	Verb
jazz it	Euphemism
jelly roll	Euphemism
Let's Adam-and-Eve-it	Euphemism
low-Greek	Euphemism
nasty	Noun
naughty	Euphemism
nookey	Noun
nooky	Noun
nub	Verb
poontang	Euphemism
punaani	Noun
punani	Noun
punanni	Noun
punni	Noun
ride	Verb
rub bellies	Euphemism
sexual intercourse	Noun
shake	Verb
the act	Euphemism

Terminology	Part of
the big F	Euphemism
tickling the fancy	Euphemism
to ball	Euphemism
tootsie roll	Euphemism
upright grand	Euphemism
wedge	Verb
woman on top	Euphemism
yum yum	Verb

Genital Sex Female Point of View

Terminology	Part of Speech
bottom's up	Euphemism
give mutton for beef	Verb
take the starch out of	Euphemism

Genital Sex Leading to Ejaculation

Terminology	Part of Speech
paradise strokes	Euphemism
short strokes	Euphemism
vinegar strokes	Euphemism

Genital Sex Male Point of View

Terminology	Part of
a bit of butt	Euphemism
a bit of fat	Euphemism
a bit of fork	Euphemism
a bit of hair	Euphemism
a bit of the old in and out	Euphemism

Terminology	Part of
a piece of fluff	Euphemism
a piece of goods	Euphemism
a piece of patch	Euphemism
a piece of skirt	Euphemism
a piece of snatch	Euphemism
a piece of stuff	Euphemism
a piece of tail	Euphemism
a poke in the whiskers	Euphemism
a poke through the whiskers	Euphemism
assault with a friendly weapon	Euphemism
bag up	Verb
bait the hook	Euphemism
balling the jack	Verb
balls deep in the furry funhouse	Euphemism
ball's eye	Euphemism
baloney hop	Euphemism
bang-bang-bang	Euphemism
bash leather	Euphemism
bat up	Euphemism
bat-foul	Verb
be in a woman's beef	Euphemism
be with a woman	Euphemism
beef in the can	Euphemism
beef injection	Euphemism
between the sheets	Euphemism
bing-bang-thank-you-mam	Euphemism
bisecting the triangle	Euphemism
bit of cunt	Euphemism
bit of flat	Euphemism
bit of fork	Euphemism
bit of front door work	Euphemism
bit of hair	Euphemism
bit of hard for a bit of soft	Euphemism

Terminology	Part of
bit of pork	Euphemism
bit of quimsy	Euphemism
bit of raspberry	Euphemism
bit of snug for a bit of stiff	Euphemism
bit of the old in and out	Euphemism
blow off loose corns	Euphemism
bludgeon on	Euphemism
board	Verb
bone-up	Euphemism
bonking	Verb
booty call	Verb
bore	Verb
break a lance with	Verb
break a peter on	Verb
break and enter	Verb
break open the pie	Verb
broad-jumping	Euphemism
bull	Verb
bumping pussy	Euphemism
bury it	Euphemism
bury the bishop	Euphemism
bury the bone	Euphemism
bury the hatchet where it won't rust	Euphemism
bury the hobbit	Euphemism
bury the wick	Euphemism
bush whack	Euphemism
bust some booty	Euphemism
bust someone out	Euphemism
butcher	Verb
buzz the Brillo	Euphemism
calk	Verb
cane	Verb
case	Verb

Terminology	Part of
caulk	Verb
changing your oil	Euphemism
chimney sweep	Euphemism
christen the yak	Euphemism
churn the butter	Euphemism
churning butter	Euphemism
churning the butter	Euphemism
coitus profundus	Verb
coochied	Verb
cure the horn	Euphemism
delivering the wood	Verb
dibble	Verb
dip one's wick	Euphemism
front door work	Euphemism
get Jack in the orchard	Verb
give a bit of hard for a bit of soft	Verb
give a bit of snug for a bit of stiff	Verb
hammer	Verb
hammering	Verb
have-one's-banana peeled	Euphemism
hole in one	Noun
hole-it	Euphemism
hose	Verb
impale	Verb
in the box	Euphemism
in to the hilt	Euphemism
introduce Charley	Euphemism
introduce the captain	Euphemism
introduce the captain to his pie	Euphemism
jab	Verb
jack	Verb
jack in the box	Euphemism
knock up	Verb

Terminology	Part of
lap clap	Euphemism
peel one's best end in	Euphemism
phallation	Noun
pin	Verb
pipe	Verb
PIV (penis in vagina)	Euphemism
plug	Verb
poke	Verb
pop it in	Euphemism
probe	Verb
prod	Verb
prong	Verb
pry open	Euphemism
pump	Verb
puncture	Verb
put it in	Euphemism
put it in and break it	Euphemism
put the devil into hell	Euphemism
ramming	Verb
rifle	Verb
rodger	Euphemism
roger	Euphemism
sink the sailor	Euphemism
sink the sausage	Euphemism
sink the soldier	Euphemism
skewer	Verb
slice of the damp	Euphemism
slip a length	Euphemism
slip her a length	Euphemism
slip one a hot beef injection	Euphemism
spike	Verb
split	Verb
spread	Verb

Terminology	Part of
stab	Verb
stick it in	Euphemism
thumb	Verb
tickling the fancy	Euphemism
tip	Verb
to get piece of ass	Euphemism
to have a piece of ass	Euphemism
to lob	Verb
tonk	Verb
tromboning	Verb
vaginate	Verb
wet one's wick	Euphemism

Kiss

Terminology	Part of Speech
biting kiss	Noun
boodle	Noun
box tonsils	Euphemism
buss	Noun
butterfly	Noun
chuck a slob	Euphemism
deep kiss	Noun
do a fade out	Euphemism
do face time	Euphemism
double butterfly	Noun
Esquimo kiss	Noun
exchange spit	Euphemism
face time	Noun
French kiss	Noun
Frenchy	Noun
give someone the works	Euphemism

Terminology	Part of Speech
give tonsil-ectomy	Euphemism
goo it	Euphemism
hang a goober	Euphemism
have some lip action	Euphemism
hickey	Noun
hot tongue	Euphemism
joining faces	Euphemism
kiss kiss	Euphemism
kissletoe	Noun
lip salute	Noun
lip sucking kiss	Noun
lip work	Euphemism
little tongue sushi	Noun
lock lips	Euphemism
Major Kiss Action	Noun
Major Lip Action	Noun
make licky face	Euphemism
make out	Euphemism
make smacky lips	Euphemism
maw	Verb
mesh	Verb
MKA	Noun
MLA	Noun
mouth wrestle	Euphemism
mouth wrestling	Noun
neck	Verb
osculate	Verb
paper kiss	Noun
pass secrets	Euphemism
PDA	Noun
peck	Verb
peck	Noun
plant a big one	Euphemism

Terminology	Part of Speech
plant a kissy poo	Euphemism
plant one	Euphemism
play smacky lips	Euphemism
play tonsil hockey	Euphemism
plonker	Noun
Public Display of Affection	Noun
pucker up	Noun
scoop	Noun
smack	Verb
smack	Noun
smack in the puss	Noun
smacker	Noun
smash mouth	Euphemism
smooch	Verb
smoodge	Verb
smooge	Verb
snog	Verb
snog	Noun
soul kiss	Noun
soul kissing	Euphemism
spit swapping	Euphemism
suck face	Euphemism
swab the tonsils	Euphemism
swapping spit	Euphemism
talking kiss	Noun
throw the tongue	Euphemism
tongue kiss	Noun
tongue kissing	Euphemism
tongue sushi	Noun
tongue wrestle	Euphemism
tonsil hockey	Noun
tonsil swab	Euphemism
trade spit	Euphemism

Terminology	Part of Speech
tulip sauce	Noun
wet kiss	Noun
wet kissing	Euphemism
wet one	Noun

Male Masturbation

Terminology	Part of Speech
a visit from Mother Fist	Euphemism
accosting the Oscar Mayer	Euphemism
activating cruise control	Euphemism
adjusting your set	Euphemism
answer the bone-a-phone	Euphemism
applying for a fishing license	Euphemism
applying the hand brake	Euphemism
arm aerobics	Euphemism
arm breaker	Euphemism
armswing	Euphemism
articulate the archdeacon	Euphemism
assault on a friendly weapon	Euphemism
attacking the one-eyed purple-headed warrior	Euphemism
auditioning the hand puppet	Euphemism
bachelor's delight	Euphemism
bachelor's fare	Euphemism
backstroke roulette	Euphemism
ball off	Euphemism
balling off	Euphemism
balls deep into your fist	Euphemism
bananas and cream	Euphemism
bang the banjo	Euphemism
bang the bishop	Euphemism

Terminology	Part of Speech
bang the wanger	Euphemism
banging the drum	Euphemism
bash the bishop	Euphemism
bash the candle	Euphemism
bash the dummy	Euphemism
batting practice	Euphemism
battling the purple-helmeted warrior	Euphemism
be you own best friend	Euphemism
beat	Verb
beat it	Euphemism
beat meat	Euphemism
beat off	Euphemism
beat one's little brother	Euphemism
beat Pete	Euphemism
beat the bald-headed bandit	Euphemism
beat the dork	Euphemism
beat the dummy	Euphemism
beat the goose	Euphemism
beat the hog	Euphemism
beat the meat	Euphemism
beat the pud	Euphemism
beat the pup	Euphemism
beat the tom-tom	Verb
beat your meat like it owes you money	Euphemism
beating it with a smile on your face	Euphemism
beating off	Euphemism
beating the bait	Euphemism
beating the bed flute	Euphemism
beating the bologna	Euphemism
beating the boner	Euphemism
beating the meat	Euphemism

Terminology	Part of Speech
beating the old man	Euphemism
beating the piss out of my best friend	Euphemism
beating the pud	Euphemism
beating the snake	Euphemism
beating the stick	Euphemism
beating your meat on the toilet seat	Euphemism
beef-stroke-it-off	Euphemism
bell polishing	Euphemism
bequeath your genes	Euphemism
biffing off	Euphemism
big date with Rosey Palms	Euphemism
big stroke time	Euphemism
bishoprage	Euphemism
blanket drill	Euphemism
bleed the goose	Euphemism
bloating the vein	Euphemism
blooch	Verb
blow off	Euphemism
blowing your own horn	Euphemism
bludgeon the beefsteak	Euphemism
blue-veined shuffle	Euphemism
bob	Verb
bob the bologna	Euphemism
bobbing the baloney	Euphemism
boffing	Verb
bologna hop	Euphemism
bombing the German helmet	Euphemism
bookend	Verb
bop	Verb
bop the baloney	Euphemism
bop the mop	Euphemism
bopping Richard	Euphemism

Terminology	Part of Speech
bopping the bishop	Euphemism
bopping the bologna	Euphemism
bopping the bonzo	Euphemism
boxing the bald champ	Euphemism
boxing the bald-headed clown	Euphemism
boxing the ballsack	Euphemism
boxing the bozack	Euphemism
boxing the clown	Euphemism
boxing with Richard	Euphemism
brandle	Verb
break one off	Euphemism
bring down	Verb
bring off by hand	Euphemism
bring oneself off	Euphemism
bring up	Verb
bringing oneself off	Euphemism
bristle up	Verb
buck the bone	Euphemism
bucking it	Euphemism
buff the dog	Euphemism
buff the mushroom	Euphemism
buff the pylon	Euphemism
buffing	Verb
buffing the banana	Euphemism
buffing the bishop	Euphemism
buffing the helmet	Euphemism
buffing the magic lamp	Euphemism
buffing the rifle	Euphemism
buffing the wood	Euphemism
buggering the hand	Euphemism
burp the baldman	Euphemism
burp the worm	Euphemism
burping the baby	Euphemism

Terminology	Part of Speech
burping the worm	Euphemism
bury the salami	Euphemism
bury the weenie	Euphemism
bust a nut	Euphemism
buttering the corn	Euphemism
butterring the muffin	Euphemism
calling all cum	Euphemism
calling down for more mayo	Euphemism
candle-stick polishing	Verb
capturing the bishop	Euphemism
carrying weight	Euphemism
cast-off	Verb
catch up with Popeye	Euphemism
catching a case of whakinitis	Euphemism
celebrating Palm Sunday	Euphemism
changing your oil	Euphemism
charge the rod	Euphemism
charm the cobra	Euphemism
charm the serpent	Euphemism
charming the snake	Euphemism
cheat the meat	Euphemism
check the oil	Euphemism
checking for impotence	Euphemism
checking for testicular cancer	Euphemism
checking the oil	Euphemism
chicken milking	Euphemism
chipping wood	Euphemism
choke hold	Euphemism
choke the bad guy	Euphemism
choke the chicken	Euphemism
choke the chook	Euphemism
choking Charlie 'till he throws up	Euphemism
choking Kojak	Euphemism

Terminology	Part of Speech
choking the bald guy until he pukes	Euphemism
choking the chipmunk	Euphemism
choking the sheriff and waiting for the posse to come	Euphemism
chong your schlong	Euphemism
churn	Verb
churn the butter	Euphemism
churning butter	Euphemism
churning the butter	Euphemism
clamming the engram	Euphemism
clamping the pipe	Euphemism
clap with one hand	Euphemism
clean the pipes	Euphemism
cleaning the rifle	Euphemism
cleaning the storm-drains	Euphemism
clearing the custard	Euphemism
clearing the snorkel	Euphemism
climbing Mount Baldy	Euphemism
climbing the tree	Euphemism
clobbering the Kleenex	Euphemism
closet frisbee	Euphemism
closing the deal	Euphemism
clubbing eddy	Euphemism
cock your shotgun	Euphemism
dilly with the willy	Euphemism
five against one	Euphemism
going blind	Verb
handball	Noun
handle	Verb
jack the beanstalk	Euphemism
jerk the mutton	Euphemism
jerking iron	Verb
juice the fruit	Euphemism

Terminology	Part of Speech
make a milkshake	Euphemism
make the bald man cry	Euphemism
milk	Verb
milk the chicken	Euphemism
pinch the cat	Euphemism
play pocket pool	Euphemism
play the bone	Euphemism
playing pocket pool	Euphemism
pocket billiards	Euphemism
pocket pinball	Euphemism
pocket polka	Euphemism
pocket pool	Euphemism
pocket waltz	Euphemism
polish the knob	Euphemism
press the button	Euphemism
prime it	Verb
pull some lumber	Euphemism
raising Lazarus from the dead	Euphemism
rub the radish	Euphemism
take down (by hand)	Euphemism
taking care of business	Euphemism
tame the bald-headed mouse	Euphemism
tromboning	Verb
tummy fuck	Euphemism
wacker	Noun
wake the dead	Euphemism
wanker	Noun
whacker	Noun
whanker	Noun

Male Virgin Sex

Terminology	Part of Speech
break a cherry	Euphemism
break in the balls	Euphemism

Oral Sex – Either

Terminology	Part of Speech
buccal intercourse	Noun
buccal onanism	Noun
coitus in ore	Noun
coitus oralis	Noun
DSL	Euphemism
Duck Sucking Lips	Euphemism
eat	Euphemism
face fucking	Euphemism
French	Euphemism
French Arts	Euphemism
French culture	Euphemism
French head job	Euphemism
French job	Euphemism
French kiss	Euphemism
French lessons	Euphemism
French love	Euphemism
French sex	Euphemism
French tricks	Euphemism
French way	Euphemism
Frenching	Euphemism
gam	Euphemism
gamahuche	Euphemism
get down	Euphemism
give a blow job	Euphemism
give a face job	Euphemism

Terminology	Part of Speech
give face	Verb
give good head	Euphemism
give head	Euphemism
give skull	Euphemism
go down on	Euphemism
go down on and do tricks	Euphemism
go for sushi	Euphemism
go south	Euphemism
head	Euphemism
head job	Euphemism
kiss it	Euphemism
kiss it down	Euphemism
kneel at the altar	Euphemism
labiate	Verb
larro	Euphemism
lay the lip	Euphemism
make mouth music	Euphemism
mouth job	Euphemism
mouth music	Euphemism
mouth-genital sex	Noun
mouthlove	Euphemism
munch	Euphemism
oragenital sex	Noun
oral coitus	Noun
oral copulation	Noun
oral erotocism	Noun
oral genitalism	Noun
oral job	Noun
oral service	Noun
oral sex	Noun
oral stimulation	Noun
oral titillation	Noun
oralism	Noun

Terminology	Part of Speech
orbit	Euphemism
orogenital sex	Noun
orogenitalism	Noun
orolabial stimulation	Noun
picnic on it	Euphemism
play mouth music	Euphemism
sit on a face	Euphemism
speak low genitalease	Euphemism
swab the tonsils	Euphemism
swing low	Euphemism
tongue fuck	Euphemism
tongue sushi	Euphemism
tongue wash	Euphemism
virilingus	Verb

Oral Sex Performed on a Female - Cunnilingus

Terminology	Part of Speech
barking at the ape	Euphemism
bikini burger	Euphemism
bird-washing	Euphemism
bite the dog end	Euphemism
blow	Verb
blow some tunes	Euphemism
box lunch	Euphemism
box lunch at the Y	Euphemism
breakfast in bed	Euphemism
brush one's teeth	Euphemism
brush teeth	Euphemism
burger munch	Euphemism
bush dinner	Euphemism
canyon yodeling	Euphemism

Terminology	Part of Speech
carpet munching	Verb
chew	Verb
chew it	Verb
chew the she-fat	Euphemism
chow box	Verb
clam dive	Euphemism
clam diving	Euphemism
clam lapping	Euphemism
clit licking	Euphemism
clitoralingus	Noun
clitus lickus	Euphemism
dive into it	Euphemism
dive into the bushes	Euphemism
doormat bashing	Verb
eat pussy	Euphemism
Frenching	Verb
fur burger	Euphemism
fur pie	Euphemism
furburger	Euphemism
fuzz burger	Euphemism
fuzzburger	Euphemism
go under the house	Euphemism
gorilla burger	Euphemism
hair pie	Euphemism
hairy pie	Euphemism
husband's supper	Euphemism
licking the beaver	Euphemism
moustache ride	Euphemism
muff pie	Euphemism
mumbling in the moss	Euphemism
one-man band	Euphemism
the feathery flick	Euphemism
tip the velvet	Euphemism

Terminology	Part of Speech
velvet buzz saw	Euphemism
whistle in the dark	Euphemism

Oral Sex Performed on a Male - Fellatio

Terminology	Part of Speech
bagpipe	Verb
bell polishing	Euphemism
bit the big one	Euphemism
bite the crank	Euphemism
biter	Noun
BJ	Euphemism
blow	Verb
blow job	Euphemism
blow my hat	Euphemism
blow my horn	Euphemism
blow off	Euphemism
blow the pipe	Euphemism
blow the whistle	Euphemism
blowing	Verb
blue jay	Euphemism
bob on the knob	Euphemism
bull by the souse	Euphemism
butterfly flick	Euphemism
cannibalize	Verb
cap	Verb
cherry flip	Euphemism
chew	Verb
chew foreskin	Euphemism
chew it	Verb
chew the goo	Euphemism
chew the slough	Euphemism

Terminology	Part of Speech
clean the pipes	Euphemism
cock bath	Euphemism
cop a doodle	Euphemism
deep throat	Euphemism
drink on a stick	Euphemism
drop on it	Euphemism
fancy lip service	Euphemism
Frenching	Verb
gargle it	Euphemism
get down on one's knees	Verb
gobble the worm	Verb
he-blow	Euphemism
hoover	Verb
hose job	Euphemism
hum job	Euphemism
knobble	Verb
kowtow chow	Euphemism
lick a prick	Verb
mouth job	Euphemism
nose to hose	Euphemism
penis mouthus	Euphemism
pipe	Verb
piston job	Euphemism
plate	Verb
playing the piccolo	Verb
polish the knob	Euphemism
prick lick	Euphemism
rooting	Verb
scarf	Verb
scarf up	Euphemism
scooby snack	Euphemism
scorf up on a bod	Euphemism
suck off	Verb

Terminology	Part of Speech
swallow the pipe	Euphemism
sword swallower	Euphemism

Oral Sex - Fellator

Terminology	Part of Speech
man-eater	Euphemism
sperm sucker	Euphemism

Oral Sex - Fellator's Mouth

Terminology	Part of Speech
coin slot	Euphemism

Oral Sex – Mutual

Terminology	Part of Speech
69	Euphemism
Alternating flame	Euphemism
Double header	Euphemism
Double marriage	Euphemism
Flip-flop	Euphemism
Fork and spoon	Euphemism
Head over heels	Euphemism
Head over heels in love	Euphemism
Loop-de-loop	Euphemism
Hoop snake	Euphemism
P's and q's	Euphemism
Playing hoop snake	Euphemism
Six-to-nine	Euphemism
Soixante-neuf	Euphemism

Terminology	Part of Speech
Vice versa	Euphemism

4. ORGASM

Female Orgasm

Terminology	Part of Speech
A-frame orgasm (Uterine orgasm)	Euphemism
Big O	Euphemism
Ring her bell (Male Point of View)	Euphemism

Male Orgasm - Ejaculation

Terminology	Part of Speech
bean spilling	Euphemism
blow off	Euphemism
blow one's fat	Euphemism
blow one's load	Euphemism
blow one's wad	Euphemism
blow up	Euphemism
bust a nut	Euphemism
bust one's gut	Euphemism
bust one's nut	Euphemism
bust your nuts	Euphemism
butter the bacon	Euphemism
butter the bacon	Euphemism
cheat the census	Euphemism
chuck	Verb
chuck the muck	Euphemism
clean the pipes	Euphemism
clear the custard	Euphemism
clearing the snorkel	Euphemism
come	Verb
come-off	Euphemism
cough cabbage water	Euphemism

Terminology	Part of Speech
crash one's muck	Euphemism
crash the yogurt truck	Euphemism
cream	Verb
cream one's jeans	Euphemism
cream one's pants	Euphemism
cue snap	Euphemism
cum	Verb
discharge	Verb
discharge the trouser mauser	Euphemism
dishonorable discharge	Euphemism
do number three	Euphemism
ease oneself	Euphemism
effect emission	Euphemism
emission	Verb
empty one's trash	Euphemism
empty the trash	Euphemism
empty the wank tank	Euphemism
fill one with come	Verb
fire a shot	Euphemism
fire blanks	Euphemism
fire in the air	Euphemism
fire your wad	Euphemism
free the tadpoles	Euphemism
get it off	Euphemism
get off	Euphemism
get one's balls off	Euphemism
get one's nuts off	Euphemism
get one's oil changed	Euphemism
get one's rocks off	Euphemism
get the upshot	Euphemism
get your gun off	Euphemism
get your nuts off	Euphemism
get your oats	Euphemism

Terminology	Part of Speech
get your rocks off	Euphemism
give one's gravy	Euphemism
go off	Euphemism
have a seminal emission	Euphemism
have a sexual reflex	Euphemism
have a spasm	Euphemism
have a sperm attack	Euphemism
have an emission	Euphemism
hive it	Euphemism
jack	Verb
jack	Verb
jack off	Euphemism
jet one's juice	Euphemism
jiffy pop	Euphemism
lose bullets	Euphemism
lose one's mess	Euphemism
lose the last round	Euphemism
number three	Euphemism
pee white	Euphemism
piss one's tallow	Euphemism
pitch	Verb
pop	Verb
pop a nut	Euphemism
pop one's cookies	Euphemism
pop one's nuts	Euphemism
pop the cork	Euphemism
ready to spit	Euphemism
seminal spurt	Euphemism
seminal vesuviation	Euphemism
send out the troops	Euphemism
shoot	Verb
shoot a wad	Euphemism
shoot bullets	Euphemism

Terminology	Part of Speech
shoot in the bush	Euphemism
shoot in the stubble	Euphemism
shoot off	Euphemism
shoot off one's load	Euphemism
shoot one's cookies	Euphemism
shoot one's cream	Euphemism
shoot one's creamy load	Euphemism
shoot one's load	Euphemism
shoot one's wad	Euphemism
shoot white	Euphemism
shoot your load	Euphemism
shooting off a load	Euphemism
shooting off the muck	Euphemism
shot his great stones	Euphemism
spermatize	Euphemism
spew	Verb
spill	Verb
spill water at a woman's feet	Euphemism
spit	Verb
splooge	Verb
spooch	Verb
spurt	Verb
squirt	Verb
squirt seed	Euphemism
squirting the seed	Euphemism
stand up and cheer	Euphemism
strain the main vein	Euphemism
strain the vein	Euphemism
throw the hash	Euphemism
throw up	Euphemism
toss beanbags	Euphemism
unload	Verb
upshoot	Verb

Terminology	Part of Speech
vesuviation	Euphemism
whitewash	Euphemism

Orgasm – Either

Terminology	Part of Speech
bang it	Euphemism
blast off	Euphemism
blow off	Euphemism
blow your top	Euphemism
bring off	Euphemism
bring someone off	Euphemism
climax	Noun
coital climax	Noun
come	Verb
come off	Euphemism
convulsion of bliss	Euphemism
crash one's muck	Euphemism
ease	Euphemism
ease nature	Euphemism
end pleasure	Euphemism
explode	Verb
get it off	Euphemism
get off	Euphemism
get one's cookies off	Euphemism
get oneself off	Euphemism
get over the mountain	Euphemism
go over the mountain	Euphemism
go to heaven	Euphemism
have a little death	Euphemism
have a sexual reflex	Euphemism
have a small stroke	Euphemism

Terminology	Part of Speech
have a spasm	Euphemism
have one's bell rung	Euphemism
have one's chimes rung	Euphemism
have one's ticket punched	Euphemism
hit the top	Euphemism
hysterical paroxysm	Euphemism
let go	Euphemism
little death	Euphemism
melt	Verb
mort douce	Euphemism
over the mountain	Euphemism
peak	Verb
peak	Noun
pleasure someone	Euphemism
pop	Verb
pop off	Euphemism
pop one's cookies	Euphemism
pop one's cork	Euphemism
pop your cookies	Euphemism
psychokick	Euphemism
reach a climax	Euphemism
reach climax	Euphemism
reach sexual climax	Euphemism
reach the big O	Euphemism
ring someone's bell	Euphemism
ring someone's chimes	Euphemism
ring the chimes	Euphemism
rock someone's world	Euphemism
satisfy oneself	Euphemism
score	Verb
see stars	Euphemism
self-gratification	Euphemism
sexual climax	Euphemism

Terminology	Part of Speech
sexual fulfillment	Euphemism
shake and shiver	Euphemism
spend	Verb
splooge	Euphemism
spooch	Euphemism
sweet agony	Euphemism
sweet death	Euphemism
take one's pleasure	Euphemism
tender agony	Euphemism
the earth moved	Euphemism
thrill	Euphemism
thrill and chill	Euphemism
top of the hill	Euphemism
UFO's	Euphemism

5. OTHER GOODIES

Menstruation

Terminology	Part of Speech
Arsenal's playing at home	Euphemism
Aunt Flo	Euphemism
Aunt Flo is here	Euphemism
Aunt Flo is visiting	Euphemism
Aunty's round	Euphemism
bad news	Euphemism
bad week	Euphemism
baker flying	Euphemism
be at number one	Euphemism
be in the Red Sea	Euphemism
be indisposed	Euphemism
be on the rag	Euphemism
be on the saddle	Euphemism
be under the weather	Euphemism
be unwell	Euphemism
become a lady	Euphemism
being hit	Euphemism
bleed	Verb
blodded park	Euphemism
bloody flag is up	Euphemism
Bloody Mary	Euphemism
call of nature	Euphemism
captain has come	Euphemism
captain is at home	Euphemism
cardinal has come	Euphemism
cardinal is come	Euphemism
carrying a bicycle seat	Euphemism
carrying the flag	Euphemism
Charlie's home	Euphemism

Terminology	Part of Speech
chase the cotton mouse	Euphemism
cherry is in sherry	Euphemism
clit clot	Euphemism
come around	Euphemism
coming on	Euphemism
country cousins	Euphemism
crimson tide	Euphemism
crimson wave	Euphemism
curse of Eve	Euphemism
d.a.	Euphemism
danger signal is up	Euphemism
decorators are in	Euphemism
dog days	Euphemism
domestic affliction	Euphemism
drop an egg	Euphemism
entertain the general	Euphemism
fall off the roof	Euphemism
falling off the roof	Euphemism
feel poorly	Euphemism
feeling unwell	Euphemism
female disorder	Euphemism
female trouble	Euphemism
feminine matters	Euphemism
field day	Euphemism
flag day	Euphemism
flag is out	Euphemism
flag is up	Euphemism
flagging	Verb
flag's out	Euphemism
flash the red flag	Euphemism
flowers	Euphemism
fly the red flag	Euphemism
flying the Japanese flag	Euphemism

Terminology	Part of Speech
flying the red flag	Euphemism
friend has come to stay	Euphemism
friends to stay	Euphemism
gals at the stockyards	Euphemism
grandma is here	Euphemism
grandma is visiting	Euphemism
grandmother has come to stay	Euphemism
hammock is swinging	Euphemism
have a caller	Euphemism
have a friend	Euphemism
have a little visitor	Euphemism
have a stomach ache	Euphemism
have a visitor	Euphemism
have it on	Euphemism
have one's aunt	Euphemism
have one's auntie with one	Euphemism
have one's granny	Euphemism
have the bends	Euphemism
have the curse	Euphemism
have the flag out	Euphemism
have the painters in	Euphemism
have the rag on	Euphemism
have the woman's complaint	Euphemism
having grandmother to stay	Euphemism
having my monthlies	Euphemism
having the painters in	Euphemism
having visitors from Redbank	Euphemism
hell week	Euphemism
high tide	Euphemism
hit by a Mack truck	Euphemism
holy week	Euphemism
immenses	Euphemism
impercolating	Euphemism

Terminology	Part of Speech
in the Red Sea	Euphemism
in the saddle	Euphemism
indisposed	Euphemism
infantry has landed	Euphemism
Kit has come	Euphemism
little friend	Euphemism
little sister	Euphemism
little visitor	Euphemism
looks like a wet weekend	Euphemism
menses	Euphemism
menstrual period	Euphemism
minge week	Euphemism
month blues	Euphemism
monthlies	Euphemism
monthly causes	Euphemism
monthly courses	Euphemism
monthly cycle	Euphemism
monthly flowers	Euphemism
monthly flux	Euphemism
monthly period	Euphemism
monthly rag	Euphemism
monthly term	Euphemism
monthly bill	Euphemism
monthly flow	Euphemism
my auntie has come	Euphemism
my country cousins have come	Euphemism
my cousins have come	Euphemism
my little friend is here	Euphemism
my little sister is here	Euphemism
my little visitor is here	Euphemism
my period	Euphemism
my relations are visiting	Euphemism
my relations have come	Euphemism

Terminology	Part of Speech
no gym this week	Euphemism
not feeling well	Euphemism
note from my mother	Euphemism
observing holy week	Euphemism
off duty	Euphemism
off games	Euphemism
off the roof	Euphemism
Old Faithful	Euphemism
on the blob	Euphemism
on the jamrag	Euphemism
on the plug	Euphemism
on the rag	Euphemism
on the saddle	Euphemism
on the white cotton horse	Euphemism
OTR	Euphemism
out of circulation	Euphemism
out of commission	Euphemism
out of order	Euphemism
period	Noun
problem day	Euphemism
put the flag out	Euphemism
rag time	Euphemism
ragging	Verb
raw burger	Euphemism
red baron	Euphemism
red dog on a white horse	Euphemism
red flag is in	Euphemism
red flag	Euphemism
red flag	Euphemism
red flag is out	Euphemism
red flag is up	Euphemism
red flag of defiance is out	Euphemism
red haired visitor	Euphemism

Terminology	Part of Speech
red river valley	Euphemism
red sails in the sunset	Euphemism
Red Sea	Euphemism
Red Sea's in	Euphemism
red tummy ache	Euphemism
ride the cotton bicycle	Euphemism
ride the cotton mouse	Euphemism
ride the cotton pony	Euphemism
ride the rag	Euphemism
ride the red horse	Euphemism
riding the crimson wave	Euphemism
riding the rag	Euphemism
road up for repairs	Euphemism
roses	Euphemism
see one's aunt	Euphemism
see one's auntie	Euphemism
see one's friend	Euphemism
snatch box is decorated with red roses	Euphemism
squirting clots	Euphemism
start bleeding	Euphemism
stomach cramps	Euphemism
stormy weather	Euphemism
stub one's toe	Euphemism
surf the crimson wave	Euphemism
surfing the crimson wave	Euphemism
tail flowers	Euphemism
Tampax time	Euphemism
terms	Euphemism
that time of month	Euphemism
the bends	Euphemism
the bloody flag is up	Euphemism
the bloody red flag is up	Euphemism

Terminology	Part of Speech
the courses	Euphemism
the cramps	Euphemism
the curse	Euphemism
the drips	Euphemism
the female complaint	Euphemism
the flood	Euphemism
the nuisance	Euphemism
the painters are in	Euphemism
the plague	Euphemism
the turns	Euphemism
the twitters	Euphemism
the vapors	Euphemism
those days of the month	Euphemism
time of the month	Euphemism
tummy ache	Euphemism
tums	Euphemism
under the weather	Euphemism
unwell	Euphemism
visit from Aunt Flo	Euphemism
visit from Flo	Euphemism
visit from my sister	Euphemism
visiting Redbank	Euphemism
visitor with red hair has come	Euphemism
wallflower week	Euphemism
wet burger	Euphemism
wet day	Euphemism
wet season	Euphemism
wet week	Euphemism
wet weekend	Euphemism
woman in her courses	Euphemism
woman's home companion	Euphemism
women's terms	Euphemism
women's thing	Euphemism

Terminology	Part of Speech
wrong time of month	Euphemism

Nudity – Either

Terminology	Part of Speech
Adam and Eve's tog	Euphemism
Adam-and-Eve-it	Euphemism
adamatical	Adjective
adamic	Adjective
adamical	Adjective
air one's pores	Euphemism
altogether	Noun
angel's suit	Euphemism
au naturel	Euphemism
bare	Adjective
bare-ass	Euphemism
bare-assed	Euphemism
bared	Verb
bare-naked	Euphemism
bare-naked and in the flesh	Euphemism
bare-skin	Euphemism
bare-skinned	Euphemism
be in a state of nature	Euphemism
be in a state of undress	Euphemism
birthday attire	Euphemism
birthday clothes	Euphemism
birthday gear	Euphemism
birthday suit	Euphemism
birth-naked	Euphemism
body-naked	Euphemism
buck naked	Euphemism
buff	Noun

Terminology	Part of Speech
buff bare	Euphemism
buff leather	Euphemism
buff skin	Euphemism
butt naked	Adjective
butt naked and in the flesh	Euphemism
in the buff	Euphemism
Let's Adam-and-Eve-it	Euphemism

Nudity – Male

Terminology	Part of Speech
Adam-like	Euphemism
Adam's clothing	Euphemism
Adam's pj's	Euphemism
bollocky-starkers	Euphemism

Sex Sounds

Terminology	Part of Speech	Gender
thunderclap	Noun	Male
unf (universal noise of fucking)	Noun	Either

Sexual Arousal

Terminology	Part of Speech	Gender
bring on	Euphemism	Either
burn up over	Euphemism	Either
burning	Verb	Either
carnal desire	Noun	Either
carry a bat for	Euphemism	Male
carry a load	Euphemism	Male

Terminology	Part of Speech	Gender
carry live ammunition	Euphemism	Male

Sexually Aroused

Terminology	Part of Speech	Gender
120 in the shade	Euphemism	Either
ache for	Euphemism	Either
aching for a side of beef	Euphemism	Male
all fussed up	Euphemism	Either
all het up	Euphemism	Either
all hot and bothered	Euphemism	Either
all sexed up	Euphemism	Either
all steamed up	Euphemism	Either
all worked up	Euphemism	Either
belly itching	Euphemism	Either
belly up	Euphemism	Either
booty-call	Euphemism	Either
cock in her eye	Euphemism	Female
hard up	Euphemism	Either
het up	Euphemism	Either
hornification	Euphemism	Either
horny	Adjective	Either
hot in the tail	Euphemism	Either
randy	Noun	Either

Vaginal Rear Entry

Terminology	Part of Speech
croupade	Noun

Vaginal Secretions

Terminology	Part of Speech
bream-cream	Euphemism
cunt juice	Euphemism
juice	Euphemism
love juice	Euphemism
vagina juice	Euphemism
vaginal juice	Euphemism

Virgin – Either

Terminology	Part of Speech
canned goods	Euphemism
green goods	Euphemism
jewel	Noun

Virgin – Female

Terminology	Part of Speech
cherry girl	Euphemism
cherry ripe	Euphemism
fresh meat	Euphemism
intact	Noun
maidenhood	Noun
rose	Noun

REFERENCES

Cosmopolitan. (2011). He Calls His Penis What?
http://www.cosmopolitan.com/sex-love/tips-
moves/words-men-use-for-their-penises

Global Language Monitor. (2012).
http://www.languagemonitor.com/

Google. (2016). www.google.com

The Language of Love, Lust, Sex. (2016). Dictionary of Sexual
Terms. www.sex-lexus.com

National Coalition for Men. (2011). 174 Ways to Call a Penis
Something Other Than a Penis.
http://ncfm.org/2011/06/activities/san-diego/174-
ways-to-call-a-penis-something-other-than-penis/

The Open Salon. (2011). 101 Words for Penis.
http://open.salon.com/blog/bobbot/2011/01/25/101
_words_for_penis

The Online Slang Dictionary. (2016).
http://onlineslangdictionary.com/

Stanford University. (2015). Slang for Penis and Testicles.
http://www.stanford.edu/~eckert/PDF/PenisTesticle
sSlang.pdf

Urban Dictionary. (2016). www.urbandictionary.com

Yahoo. (2015). How Many Different Words Can You Come Up
with for Penis?
http://answers.yahoo.com/question/index?qid=20080
109160814AAEzeTY

ABOUT THE AUTHOR

My pen name is Teesa Mee, but friends and family call me Terrie. I was born and raised in Southwest Detroit and lived there until I married in 1979. Unable to have children, we adopted our son through Toledo, OH Catholic Social Services in 1984. In 1986, I won the "Missing Case of Miller Light" hidden in Detroit. The $10,000 prize gave us the means to adopt our daughter from Seoul, South Korea in 1987.

My world nearly ended when our son hung himself in our garage in February 2008. He was four months shy of his 25th birthday when his struggle with bipolar disorder and borderline personality disorder ended. However, my struggle as a survivor was just beginning. After finding hope with a local Survivors of Suicide group, I now do public speaking on behalf of survivors and share with others dealing with suicide, especially other parents.

I finally completed my BS IT in Web Development in June 2015, but instead of following that career path, I began an editing career as Indie Editing Services. I get to use my love of reading to earn a living, while helping authors create their best books. In addition to contributing to the anthologies This Beautiful Escape, Warrior Women, and Detours in Our Destinations, I have published a book of poetry, Looking Back: Poems from My Adolescent Self, as well as Thesaurus Erotica.

You can follow me on Facebook at
https://www.facebook.com/teesa.mee.1

Or you can like my Facebook Author Page at
https://www.facebook.com/AuthorTeesaMee

On Goodreads at
https://www.goodreads.com/author/show/13886161.Teesa_Mee

On Twitter at https://twitter.com/TeesaMee

On Amazon at http:// amazon.com/Teesa-Mee/e/B01FIOU4QM.

You can find my editing business on Facebook at www.facebook.com/indieproofreaders and on the web at www.indieeditingservices.com.

www.ingramcontent.com/pod-product-compliance
Lightning Source LLC
Chambersburg PA
CBHW060335290526
45793CB00003B/624